YORK NOT

General Editors: Professor
of Stirling) & Professor Su
University of Beirut)

W. H. Auden

SELECTED POEMS

Notes by Dominic Hyland

MA (CAMBRIDGE) M ED (MANCHESTER)
Tutor Counsellor with the Open University

**LONGMAN
YORK PRESS**

Extracts from *Selected Poems of W.H. Auden* by W.H. Auden, edited by
Edward Mendelson, are reprinted by kind permission of Faber and Faber
Ltd, London.

In the U.S.A. these extracts are from *W.H. Auden: Collected Poems*,
edited by Edward Mendelson, and are reprinted by kind permission of
Random House, Inc., New York. Copyright © 1976 by Edward Mendelson,
William Meredith and Monroe K. Spears, Executors of the Estate of W.H.
Auden.

YORK PRESS
Immeuble Esseily, Place Riad Solh, Beirut.

LONGMAN GROUP UK LIMITED
Longman House, Burnt Mill, Harlow,
Essex CM20 2JE, England
Associated companies, branches and representatives
throughout the world

© Librairie du Liban 1985

First published 1985
Third impression 1990

ISBN 0-582-79253-3

Produced by Longman Group (FE) Ltd.
Printed in Hong Kong

Contents

Part 1

Introduction

The life of W.H. Auden

Wystan Hugh Auden was born in York on 21 February 1907. His
father was a scientist, and for a long time Auden's own interests were
in that field of knowledge. At school, for example, he specialised in
biology, and his great friend, Christopher Isherwood (*b.* 1904), tells us
that 'his playbox was full of thick scientific books on geology and
metals and machines'* Auden's mother was the daughter of the Vicar
of Wroxham in Norfolk, the Rev. R.H. Bicknell, and it may have been
her influence that gave Auden a religious instinct that stayed with him
throughout his life. The family, indeed, had a strong religious back-
ground for both Auden's grandfathers had been Church of England
clergymen. With this in mind, it is not surprising to learn that the
household was a strict one.

At the age of eight Wystan was sent to a school in Surrey. The family
were living in Birmingham at the time, so this was a considerable
separation. The school, St Edmund's at Hindhead, was a religious
foundation to which his two brothers, Bernard and John, had also
been sent. John was still there in 1915 when Wystan arrived. It was here
that Wystan met his life-long friend, Christopher Isherwood, who tells
us that at this time the young Auden was podgy, and white-faced. He
achieved academic and social success at that school before he was
moved, after five years, to Norfolk. There he went to Gresham's
School in Holt, and he offers the following not very flattering description of himself at this period of his life:

> The son of book-loving, Anglo-Catholic parents of the professional
> class, the youngest of three brothers, I was . . . mentally precocious,
> physically backward, short-sighted, a rabbit at all games, very
> untidy and grubby, a nail biter, a physical coward, dishonest, senti-
> mental, with no community sense whatsoever, in fact a typical little
> highbrow and difficult child.

Auden did not particularly enjoy Gresham's School where, he said,
'the whole of our moral life was based on fear,' but he was successful

* Christopher Isherwood, *Lions and Shadows*, Hogarth Press, London, 1938, p.48.

there. In 1925 he won a scholarship to study natural science at Christ Church at Oxford. But once at Oxford, he changed the subject of his studies from natural science to English literature. At Oxford he met and worked (for instance, on *Oxford Poetry*) with others who were to become significant poets, people such as Stephen Spender (*b.* 1909), Cecil Day Lewis (1904–72) and Louis MacNeice (1907–63). Christopher Isherwood gives the following description of Auden, aged eighteen:

> I found him very little changed. True, he had grown enormously; but his small, pale yellow eyes were still screwed painfully together in the same short-sighted scowl and his stumpy immature fingers were still nail bitten and stained—nicotine was mixed with ink. He was expensively but untidily dressed in a chocolate-brown suit which needed pressing, complete with one of the new fashionable double-breasted waistcoats.*

It was to Christopher Isherwood that Auden dedicated a small volume of poems which he produced in 1928 in his third year at Oxford. The poems were published in a very limited edition; there were just forty-five copies printed and the printing was initially done by hand by Stephen Spender. This was not, however, Auden's first venture in publishing poetry. He had edited two volumes of verse in 1926 and 1927 which he entitled *Oxford Poetry*. His editorial to the 1926 volume highlights his insistence on making poetry relevant to real living, a feature which is to characterise all his poetic endeavour; he says:

> We would suggest that poetry which does not at least attempt to face the circumstances of its time may supply charming holiday reading but vital interest, anything strictly *poetic*, it certainly will not. If it is a natural preference to inhabit a room with casements opening upon Fairyland, one at least of them should open upon the Waste Land.

The last two words there refer to the great poem by T.S. Eliot (1888–1965) which had appeared in 1922. It is a disturbing poem dealing with the threat to civilisation as we know it. Auden had a great respect for Eliot's work.

Whilst at Oxford, Auden immersed himself in literature—though he only gained a third-class degree in the subject. He spent the year 1928–9 in Berlin in order to learn German. Here he fell under the influence of a school of psychology owing much to Sigmund Freud (1856–1939). You will find that in his poetry there is an insistence on the need to look as much into the mind of man as into his heart. At this

* In *Lions and Shadows*, 1938, p.60.

time Auden also came under the influence of the German dramatist Bertolt Brecht (1898–1956), and later in his career he was to work with him on an adaptation of *The Duchess of Malfi*, a play by the English dramatist John Webster (1580–1638).

After his year in Berlin, Auden returned to England and took up a teaching post at Larchfield Academy in Scotland, and later at The Downs School in a place called Colwall in England. He enjoyed teaching and has these comments to make on the profession:

> For a teacher to be of real value to his pupils, he must be a mature and above all a happy person, giving the young the feeling that adult life is infinitely more exciting than their own; he must be prepared to give them all his powers of affection and imaginative understanding when they want them . . . *

Meanwhile Auden was intensely busy with his poetic work. In 1930 he produced the volume, entitled *Poems*, dedicated to Christopher Isherwood, some of which appears in our set text here (numbers 1 to 11) (see 'A note on the text', p.12). He revised this volume in 1932. In the revised volume he dropped seven poems from the 1930 edition and replaced them by seven others. Three of the poems in our set text are from this revised edition.

Between 1930 and 1933 Auden produced a book of poetry which he entitled *The Orators*, published in 1932. It is of some interest to learn that he had intended to publish with it a preface in which he apologised for obscurities within the book, but T.S. Eliot persuaded him to remove this preface. Stephen Spender described the work as 'one of Auden's most vital, but also his most cynical, gangish and brutal works'. Two of the poems in *Selected Poems* are from *The Orators* (numbers 15 and 16).

Auden's dramatic interests at this time found their expression in his involvement with a theatrical group called, simply, the Group Theatre. The aims of the Group were to produce plays which would have a social impact. One play they produced in 1935 was T.S. Eliot's *Murder in the Cathedral*. Auden and his friend Christopher Isherwood wrote a play called *The Dog Beneath the Skin* for the Group. It did not gain any real critical acclaim, though it was said to be better than an earlier play by Auden for the Group Theatre, called *The Dance of Death* (1934). He and Isherwood also collaborated in the writing of *The Ascent of F6, A Tragedy in Two Acts* which was produced in 1936. The composer Benjamin Britten (1913–76) provided the music for this and other compositions by Auden and was a life-long friend who, according to Auden had a 'extraordinary musical sensibility in relation to the

---

* In *The Old School*, ed. Graham Greene, Cape, London, 1934, p.103.

English language'. They worked together with the GPO Film Unit about this time, producing publicity for the Unit. Auden's well-known poem 'The Night Mail' dates from this period; it formed the final section of the documentary film *Night Mail*. This was a time in Auden's life when he travelled a good deal. In 1936, for instance, he went to Iceland; two of the poems in *Selected Poems* are taken from his *Letters from Iceland* (1937). In 1937 he travelled to Spain. The Spanish Civil War had broken out in 1936 and Auden sympathised with the Left-wing element in the conflict. Many writers and artists from outside Spain joined what was called the International Brigade. Auden offered himself as an ambulance driver. He never proved himself a hero on this short-lived expedition; indeed it was a failure, and he only remained in Spain for a few weeks. In his poem 'Spain' (number 34) in *Selected Poems* he describes it as: 'that arid square, that fragment nipped off from hot/Africa'. This is not particularly inspiring poetry —but then Auden seems to have been disillusioned by what he experienced there. The following year, 1938, he resumed his travels; this time he went to China with Christopher Isherwood, on a more protracted visit lasting six months. They had been commissioned to write a travel book together. The book came to be called *Journey to a War* (1938) and extracts from it are to be found as number 40 in our set text. The Japanese were at this time invading China, and Auden and Isherwood insisted on witnessing the conflict at first hand. His reflections on war, poem number 40, are universalised beyond the particular conflict in China to the suffering in evidence, too, elsewhere in the world:

And maps can really point to places
Where life is evil now:
Nanking; Dachau.

Four months after his return from China, Auden was on his travels again. This time, he and Isherwood were bound for America where they intended to live for the rest of their lives.

This decision on Auden's part attracted a great deal of hostile criticism: he was accused of being unpatriotic, of escaping from Europe when it was threatened by war. There were those, though, who defended his integrity as an artist, claiming that he had a right to choose to work where he could work best. Auden fell in love with America, and at the end of the war acquired United States citizenship. He was widely acclaimed in universities and other establishments of learning there, and was given such public honours as the Pulitzer Prize in May 1948, and the Bollingen Prize in 1953. The following year he was elected to the American Academy of Arts and Letters. His appearance, despite all this success, had not altered much. Anthony Hecht, the American poet, described him (in 1950) in these terms:

He was remarkably myopic and could rarely recognise anyone at a distance of more than ten feet. His clothing . . . resembled, in his own words, 'an unmade bed'.*

Auden's volume of poetry *The Shield of Achilles* (1955), selections from which are to be found in *Selected Poems* (numbers 70 to 75), won him a National Book Award, and the following year he was elected to the post of Professor of Poetry at the University of Oxford. He had well and truly achieved those 'glittering prizes' of which he had written all those years ago in his poem 'Oxford' (1940). He was to be closely connected with Oxford for the rest of his life, being elected a Fellow of his old College, Christ Church, in 1962. In a collection of essays called *The Dyer's Hand* published in 1963, Auden had this to say about modern poetry:†

The characteristic style of 'Modern' poetry is an intimate tone of voice, the speech of one person addressing one person, not a large audience; whenever a modern poet raises his voice he sounds phony.

The influence of his years in America is revealed in that final word.

Auden's truly final word, however, was to be published after his death. A volume of poems called *Thank you, Fog* appeared in 1974. Auden had died in Vienna, on 28 September 1973. Read poem number 99 and you will find his own brief summary of his poetic career. The last stanza of that poem possibly introduces an aspect of Auden's life that has been largely neglected here, namely his return to religion. Though he was born into a religious family he briefly lost his faith. Gradually, however, he returned to his Anglo-Catholicism, and much of his post-1930's poetry is based on a Christian view of life. At the same time, it can never be claimed that Auden was totally orthodox in any way. We have seen some of the many references to his eccentric appearance. He was not easily classified. He was a man, for example, who gladly married a woman without any intention of living with her. Erika Mann, the eldest daughter of the famous German writer Thomas Mann (1956–1941), was being persecuted by the National Socialist Party in Germany, and needed to leave Germany. One solution she thought of was that of marrying an Englishman and thereby claiming British citizenship. It is said that she asked Christopher Isherwood to marry her and he refused. He did suggest Auden, though, and Auden was pleased to oblige. They were married in 1935 and remained married even though they never lived together.

---

* In an article 'Discovering Auden', *The Harvard Advocate*; quoted by Charles Osborne, *W.H. Auden, The Life of a Poet*, Eyre Methuen, London, 1980, p.233.
† *The Dyer's hand*, Faber and Faber, London, 1963.

The literary and historical background

Auden owed his inspiration in his first writings to the American-born poet T.S. Eliot. Eliot had published his poem *The Waste Land* in 1922. This poem was to undergo revisions in subsequent years and would lose and acquire sections according to the poet's will or whim. This technique helps to explain one of the difficulties in reading Auden's poems in the present selection, since he adopted the method of producing poems separately and then incorporating them in longer works. Like Eliot, he used his poetry in his early work to convey a sense of doom, of the loss of civilisation. Eliot's verse has often been accused of being obscure and the same charge was levelled at much of the verse written by Auden and published in the early 1930s. (Reference has been made earlier to Eliot's advice to him *not* to include a preface apologising for the obscurities within the poems.)

The 1930s produced a group of intellectual, Left-wing poets. They were committed to rousing the public conscience whether on a political or social level. This is how one of them, Stephen Spender, described them:

> We anti-Fascist writers of what has been called the Pink Decade were not, in any obvious sense, a lost generation. But we were divided between our literary vocation and an urge to save the world from Fascism. We were the Divided Generation of Hamlets who found the world out of joint and failed to set it right. The call we heard was by no means so absurd as it may sound to a later generation. For in those days, Japan could still have been prevented from invading Manchuria, Hitler could have been thrown out of the Anschluss or the invasion of the Rhineland, the Spanish Republic could have been saved. If any of these opportunities had been seized, there would have been no terrible totalitarian war followed by a totalitarian peace: the one thing required then was a conscience ... *

The poet is referring in his phrase 'Pink Decade' to the charge made against them that they were Communist sympathisers (red is the colour of international Communism, pink a fainter shade of red). Fascism describes a political movement on the Right wing of politics, particularly evident in the Europe of the time in Germany, Italy and Spain. It was to Spain that Auden had gone in 1937 to help to oppose Fascism – a mission which was to prove a fiasco.

The extract from Stephen Spender quoted above refers to the outbreak of a larger conflict than the Spanish civil war, namely the Second World War. The same topic is treated in a poem by one of the other

* Stephen Spender, *World Within World*, Hamish Hamilton, London, 1951, p.202.

poets of this period, C. Day Lewis. In his poem 'Newsreel' he talks of the cinema audience being lulled into apathy as they sit and passively watch the screen. He describes the cinema as a 'dream house'. One day the dream of what is presented on film will be shattered by reality:

See the big guns, rising, groping, erected
To plant death in your world's soft womb,
Fire-bud, smoke-blossom, iron seed projected—
Are these exotics? They will grow nearer home:

Grow nearer home—and out of the dream-house stumbling
One night into a strangling air and the flung
Rage of children and thunder of stone niagaras tumbling,
You'll know you slept too long.

Louis MacNeice in his poem *Autumn Journal* (1938) talks of 'the national conscience, creeping,/seeping through the night'. But the efforts at rousing the national conscience did not succeed in warding off the Second World War. And that war effectively changed the society that these poets had known and wished to preserve. Auden speaks of the despair that he and his fellows felt at the advance of the catastrophe that would so shatter the world. In the last stanza of his poem, 'September 1, 1939', he tells us that

Defenceless under the night
Our world in stupor lies.

It is typical of the man that, even given the hopelessness of the situation, he can still give voice to optimism and (in the final line) 'Show an affirming flame'.

Even in 1968 in his poem 'Ode to Terminus' Auden still gives voice to such optimism, despite his awareness that he belongs to a 'plundered and poisoned' world. The last part of the following extract attacks those poets who would not face the social and political reality and speak the truth. Auden and his 'gang', as they were sometimes called, always boasted of offering a poetic voice in a world where 'things fall apart'.

In this world our colossal immodesty
has plundered and poisoned, it is possible
    You still might save us, who by now have
    learned this: that scientists, to be truthful,

must remind us to take all they say as a
tall story, that abhorred in the Heav'ns are all
    self-proclaimed poets who, to wow an
    audience, utter some resonant lie.

A note on the text

The poems dealt with in these Notes are to be found in *Selected Poems*, edited by Edward Mendelson and first published by Faber and Faber, London and Boston, in 1979.

This selection includes poems chosen from all of Auden's books of verse from 1930 to 1974. In each instance the texts of the poems are those of the first publication in book form. Some of the poems included in this text were excluded by Auden himself in later collections of his po ms. Others he revised and changed in a variety of ways. The poems are arranged in chronological order and there is a useful date reference appended to each of the poems.

Part 2

Summaries
of SELECTED POEMS

It was Easter as I walked in the public gardens   (8:1)

SUMMARY: Auden depicts himself as walking through a park and being attracted by the beauty of nature and the promise of new life. Then suddenly he comes across a much less attractive scene—a man on his own who appears to be in considerable distress. The sight of this man reminds him of the universal fact that before we can have life something must die. Then there come, too, to his mind, memories of less happy days, memories not only of death but also of simple misery. The rest of the day holds visions of sadness and even failure. The poem does seem to end on a lighter note within the refreshing shower that falls, but even this leads to a fairly pessimistic view of existence.

COMMENTARY: The poem was written in April 1929 and is referred to in Auden's *Collected Poetry* as '1929'.

The Easter image with which it opens suggests promise—the return of life to the earth. Auden sees evidence of the beauty of nature in the 'frogs exhaling from the pond' or the 'traffic of magnificent cloud'. Everything seems at peace, or, as the poet puts it, 'without anxiety'.

The poet is equated with the spring lover who finds 'an altering speech for altering things'—a phrase which neatly exemplifies Auden's fondness for the well-turned phrase. Things are bursting into life and feel a 'fresh power'. These opening lines gain their impact by the strong contrast that is offered in the next part of the poem. Auden looks for the dramatic effect and it is achieved here by the sudden presentation of distress. The image he uses to describe the 'solitary man' is startling. He sits there, in shape and appearance as 'helpless and ugly as an embryo chicken'. We can conjecture that Auden intended a certain irony in his image. Easter is, after all, a season often depicted by the image of the broken shell and the emerging chick. There, though, the chick is yellow and fluffy and pretty. Here it is in its raw and ugly state. The beginnings of life are, after all, Auden suggests, often associated with unattractive realities.

He moves in this section to reflections on his own inadequacies by comparison with the fruitful experiences of some of his friends. He sees little promise there, little hope of personal fruition. Everything begins to assume the same hopeless air. So it is that he uses the 'fallen bicycles' to enhance the effect of hopelessness. It is easy to see that the image could have been employed to give an effect of happy abandonment, for example. The bicyles could have been evidence of a wish to live life to the full. Instead, Auden uses them to suggest death again. There were no happy sounds to disturb what he calls 'the sessile hush'. The word 'sessile' is a botanical term and describes a natural phenomenon where a flower, for example, has no stalk but is attached directly to its base. Auden's use of the image is rather obscure. Perhaps he regarded that kind of growth as less attractive than, say, the proud display of beauty from stemmed flowers. Thus, the 'hush' would have an equally unattractive effect. The 'swept gown ends of a gesture' refers to the long dresses that would be lifted slightly to avoid contact. This kind of action would betoken more life. But it is absent.

Absent, too, is any sense of joy that might be occasioned by the 'sudden shower' that is mentioned. The image is connected with a further obscurity occurring in the last line: 'Making choice seem a necessary error'. It is useful to link this thought with the idea that the shower 'fell willingly', which suggests that there is in nature some evidence of the exercise of choice. Auden toys with the philosophical idea that free will, though apparently a problem in existence, is an essential part of nature. Some may see it as some kind of mistaken notion, but its presence is what makes us human.

It is time for the destruction of error   (8:IV)

SUMMARY: The time for what Auden calls 'the destruction of error' has come. Idyllic summer afternoons are over, hopes of a better life are abandoned as people await the inevitable.

Nature is in tune with the loss of hope, as shown in the 'falling leaves'. And children at play see plenty of evidence of the doom in store.

The enemy at large is under orders to destroy all suggestions of originality and to put in its place uniform conformity. The poet and his friend realise what love really means. It is not a superficial, passing feeling. They know that love needs the evidence of death, needs to demonstrate that love can, in some way, survive even death.

COMMENTARY: The opening line of this poem depends for understanding on the interpretation of the word 'error' in the last line of the previous poem. So the 'error', indicating 'free will', has to be exterminated. Any evidence of its existence must be removed. The chairs in the garden, in the second line of this poem, represent that freedom to talk and to discuss openly, a notion that is continued in the third line.

A sense of violence is introduced in the mention of 'storms' in line 4. The reference to 'sanatoriums' in the line that follows suggests that, in

Auden's mind, there is a place in society for these institutions. They represent the belief that the mind of man matters, that the possibility for cure must always be there, that optimism is vital. But the human spirit is under threat.

The innocent forms of nature recognise the imminence of disaster. Auden's images of the 'fuming alkali-tip' and 'the flooded football ground' demonstrate ironically that the children are already intimately connected with these various forms of threat. Their 'dragons' are not mythical, they are real.

The menace, Auden tells us, is not always so visible. We will meet frequent 'spy' images in his poetry and they appear in this section of the poem in his talk of 'constant whisper and the casual question'. It is the business of these evil agents to destroy all semblance of individuality and freedom. Auden's language here is forbidding—'destroy', 'enforce', 'censor', 'organised fear'. Man will become not a thinking being but an 'articulated skeleton'.

The last section of the poem contains some further examples of the obscurity of some of Auden's verse. The obscurity arises from compression of ideas. It is difficult, therefore, to guess exactly what is meant by such a phrase as 'The self-confidence of the falling root'. The gist of this section of the poem is clear enough. The poet intends to convey that the persistence of love will provide the only justification for seeing people as human. The so-called death of such lovers will provide an inspiration to others and, as such, will bear fruit. So it will be like the 'death of the grain', which will fall into the earth and produce its own fruit.

Those who could not experience true love will never be so fruitful. Auden gives an instance of this in the image of 'the hard bitch' who could give no love and experience none. She was 'stiff' and barren when alive. She will remain as unproductive on her death. Only those who led lives which had a sense of purpose and meaning could hope to continue to make contributions to humanity, despite the discouraging effects of the tyranny that is threatening.

Look, stranger, at this island now (27)

SUMMARY: The first stanza of the poem invites the reader to admire the visual and aural beauties of the island. The light is clean, the sound of the sea rhythmical and pleasing.

The second stanza depicts the poet and his reader poised on the edge of a cliff. The white face of the cliff reaches down to the sea's edge. As they look down on the sea, they can hear the tide washing noisily against the base of the cliff. They watch a lone sea-bird alight for a moment on the cliff-face, and then fly off again.

The third and final stanza creates a picture of distant ships all going about their business. Auden likens them first to 'floating seeds' and then to clouds. He says they may well both become parts of our memories, when we recall such idyllic days.

COMMENTARY: The lilting nature of the verse in the opening stanza of the poem amply demonstrates the delight Auden wishes to portray. The abundance of soft, liquid 'l' sounds in this stanza is part of the idyll he wishes to create. He invites his reader to enjoy the luxury of sight and sound.

The island here can be taken literally to represent England, or it can be seen figuratively as representing any 'stable' state. Again, there is another interpretation of the image which suggests it can stand for a selfish form of existence—an insularity which cares nothing for others.

An examination of the second stanza may help to resolve these conflicting interpretations. The sound and visual effects of this second stanza closely resemble similar effects achieved in the poem 'Dover Beach' by the Victorian poet Matthew Arnold (1822–88):

> the cliffs of England stand,
> Glimmering and vast, out in the tranquil bay.
> Come to the window, sweet is the night-air!
> Only, from the long line of spray
> Where the sea meets the moon-blanch'd sand,
> Listen! you hear the grating roar
> Of pebbles which the waves draw back and fling,
> At their return, up the high strand . . .

The invitation in that third line 'Come to the window' helps to 'place' the reader. The poet and he are together. It is the same effect that Auden gains in the first line of his poem where he tells us that they are 'Here at the small field's ending'. Arnold paints a clear picture of what can be seen, and heard and even smelled—'sweet is the night air'. The same aural effect of the wash of the pebbles on the beach is caught in both poets' work. The versification which helps simulate the movement of the sea and the shingle is similar, too, in both works.

In Arnold's poem, the reference is decidedly to an English scene. He is concerned about the threat of decadence in England and the loss of faith and meaning in life. Auden's use of similar visual and aural effects, the close resemblance in the verse forms, all persuade us that his poem is also about England. He is not trying, within this single poem, to philosophise about existence in general terms. Arnold goes on to use his poem for that kind of purpose, but Auden in his final stanza continues his description of an idyllic scene.

In his use of the word 'voluntary' in the last stanza there is just a suggestion of his concern that exercise of free will should be applauded and encouraged. It would be in keeping, say, with the spirit of the poems already examined here. But Auden's own more 'urgent' intention is to create a rich sense of enjoyment at the view of this typical English scene.

The second stanza shows the poet at work 'for your delight'. The constant movement is created by such words as 'falls', and 'scrambles', as well as by images that suggest rest from movement like that of the gull lodging on the side of the cliff. The movement is reflected in the shape of the verse: none of the lines are end-stopped, for instance. Look at the way in which the word 'sucking' is divided between one line and another thereby creating a visual image of itself. The last part of the word is sucked, as it were, into the first part of the next line.

The constant use of harsh consonants in such words as 'pluck', 'knock', 'scrambles', 'sucking' helps create the resistance or opposition to force as well as the forcefulness itself. The final stanza is quiet by contrast. The silence of the 'floating seeds' is enhanced by the whole view having an unreal quality. The objects are as though seen in memory only, or, at another remove, as though in a mirror (Auden refers to 'the harbour mirror'). The sea must be calm to create this mirror effect, and the sense of an untroubled atmosphere is evident in that last, lingering line with its long vowel sounds: 'And all the summer through the water saunter'.

'Spain' (34)

SUMMARY: The opening stanza of the poem begins with a statement, it seems, of the obvious: 'Yesterday all the past'. In fact, it is a very succinct way of saying that the history of Spain up to the present has been an emphasis on what *has* been achieved. So, the first line goes on to suggest that the main concern had been for expansion, the acquisition of trade-routes which could add to the 'size' of Spain. The emphasis was on building the empire. It brought the spread of materialism (the 'counting-frame') and civilisation, too, but also of death ('the cromlech').

The second stanza talks, too, of initial gains made, of arts and skills developed, of further prosperity and expansion. The third stanza talks of the coming of reality, of replacing the myths and legends of other lands by the conquerors who built their fortresses there. Instead of those ancient myths they provided their own in the form of Christianity. The fourth stanza talks of the extreme lengths to which fanaticism would go—the trials of heretics and of witches. The poet speaks, too, of the all-embracing influence of religion in Spain 'yesterday'. It is at this point that he introduces the urgent matter of today—namely 'the struggle'—the revolution. Stanza five tells of the industrial developments that had been achieved both in Spain and within her colonies. It speaks of how education had been brought to the people. The sixth stanza focuses on cultural values, on the flowering of the theatre, for example.

It is at this stage that Auden brings things up to the present and the direct speech passages that occur in the following eight stanzas represent the cries for help from all quarters. The fifteenth stanza speaks of the response to those cries for help. People living in other lands, in remote islands, or in the 'heart of the city' swarmed towards Spain. The sixteenth stanza creates the dramatic picture of people crowded into trains and ships making their way there. Others trudged on foot. All of them, says Auden, offered their lives.

The seventeenth stanza draws that verbal map of Spain which Auden sees as an 'arid square' separated from the African continent but linked roughly to Europe. There, he says, the principles of these many supporters of Spain take physical shape. The stanza continues into the eighteenth with this notion of emotions now materialising. The feelings of fear that drive people to seek a cure for ill-health or look for a more pleasing climate to help them to escape hardship are now effective in driving men to form armies to ward off the political evils that face Spain. Emotions of greed are encapsulated in open physical violence expressed by such things as bombs or firing-squads. Emotions of pity and sympathy find expression in the presence of 'the ambulance and the sandbag'.

The outcome of all this, Auden suggests in the twentieth stanza, might be a promising and fruitful future. There will be research done on the question, he says, of 'fatigue/And the movements of packers'. There may be a hint of facetiousness in this. The reference seems to be what is known as 'time-and-motion' study which aims to improve efficiency. However, it may be that Auden is stressing the humanitarian aspects of such research. Other forms of research may concentrate on the effects of radiation, or the improvement of health and awareness by dietary methods.

The next stanza, twenty-one, talks of the joys of true freedom, of being able to do what one pleases, trivial or otherwise. This freedom to enjoy music, to pursue hobbies, and, as he says in stanza twenty-two, to exercise simple democratic methods such as

> The eager election of chairmen
> By the sudden forest of hands.

The twenty-third stanza talks of poets blossoming forth, producing a great flowering of poetry (rather ironically, considering the war, Auden uses a 'bomb' image to express this idea). People will be free to stroll and travel the streets without any fear of reprisal.

That, however, is the future. In stanza twenty-four, there is the reality of death, of being even involved in doing the killing. There is mention of the work of the propagandist ('the flat ephemeral pamphlet') and of having to attend tedious meetings to organise resistance and to make plans. The penultimate stanza, twenty-five, is about those directly involved in the fighting. They have to get along as best they can. Often, if someone is killed, they offer one another consolation which is necessarily brief and unsatisfactory. This is true, too, of the rushed farewells they often have to make before they go into battle. The humour is coarse and unrefined, when they look for light relief, and other distractions, like that of music, have to be improvised only. The final stanza does not offer any real hope. Instead, Auden faces the fact that there can only be one victor in such a conflict and that there will be little consolation for those who lose!

COMMENTARY: The poem has been spoken of as Auden's 'most famous political poem'—a rather large claim. The form the poem takes reflects something of the struggle which one assumes he wishes to portray. There is the balance of past and present, in which the poet seems to be attempting to show how one is struggling with the other. The forces of reaction (those who support the past) are in conflict with those of progress. The first six stanzas outline the achievements and failings of the past. They read rather like a catalogue of historic events. In the fourth, fifth and sixth stanzas he intrudes the suggestion of conflict in a brief phrase: 'but today the struggle'. It is only with the seventh stanza that the 'struggle' begins to find a voice.

The style of the poem up to this point has been compressed but quite clear in meaning. The references to expansion of the empire, to colonisation, to religion and persecution, to invention and education and culture have all been quite clear. With the onset of the struggle the language and expression become somewhat obscure. The pleas that are offered up on behalf of Spain are examples of Auden's deliberate introduction of the dramatic into his verse. This sense of drama is enhanced by the subsequent stanzas where he depicts the sudden call to arms of people from all over the world. The reference, no doubt, is to the forming of the International Brigade to fight on behalf of the Spanish Republicans. Auden himself travelled to Spain to lend his support. His major contribution was as a propagandist; he never fought. And what he thought of the usefulness of propaganda is expressed in his image of 'the flat ephemeral pamphlet'. The meaning of 'flat' in this context is uninspiring, colourless, insipid and lacking life.

He tries to bring his own poem to life and reality by his customary use of the banal and ordinary. As he talks of the conflict and the fear, he relates it to such everyday things as the advertisement or the holiday brochure, or to advice on breeding dogs. This is a feature that occurs earlier in the poem, in his references to such things as 'dynamos and turbines,/The construction of railways'. The conversational tone adopted in those imagined pleas and responses are part of the plainness that he wishes to simulate. And yet this ordinariness is juxtaposed to such obscurity as the phrase 'where the loose waterfall sings compact, or upright/On the crag by the leaning tower.' Fortunately obscurity is not a key feature of this poem where Auden obviously wishes to make his points clearly. He is examining the future of a nation. The result of that conflict was seen at the time as being important, since failure to oppose the rise of Fascism in Spain would have international repercussions. The final stanza seems to anticipate more than the possibility of such failure.

NOTES AND GLOSSARY:

diffusion:	spreading
cromlech:	ancient tomb
gargoyles:	ugly water-spouts, usually with an animal or human face, projecting from the walls of medieval buildings
trials of heretics:	probably a reference to the Spanish Inquisition, a Church court that tried those who taught doctrines contrary to orthodox beliefs
Sabbath of witches:	a midnight meeting of the devil and witches
bacillus:	a source of disease
Jupiter:	the largest planet in the solar system (Auden is predicting its possible destruction)
burrs:	clinging seeds
soldered:	literally, joined by a piece of melted metal
ephemeral:	passing, short-lived (Auden says the propaganda leaflet soon loses its effectiveness)

'Musée des Beaux Arts'   (42)

SUMMARY: The poem appears to have been written in the museum which gives the poem its title. The poet is looking at a painting entitled 'Icarus' by the painter Pieter Brueghel (1525−69). As he looks at the painting he reflects on the nature of pain and suffering. He sees them as having an essential place in the order of human existence, so much so that we take them for granted. The old painter recognised this instinctively. The greatest disasters can occur even whilst one is occupied with the ordinary things of life. Miracles can be awaited even if some are indifferent to them. Savagery and inhumanity are an integral part of human existence and can find expression just as naturally as even the most basic functions in the animal world. Brueghel's painting depicts just such a combination of the wonderful and the ordinary. Icarus, the son of Daedalus, escaped from Crete, according to Greek mythology, by using wings of feather and wax. Sadly, he flew too close to the sun; the heat melted the wax, and he plunged into the sea. The painting shows Icarus disappearing into the sea—all that is to be seen of him are his legs sticking upright out of the water! All around, the ordinary things of life continue. A farmer continues to plough his field. A ship, which may well have witnessed the fatality, passes by on urgent business.

COMMENTARY: The matter-of-fact attitude, the juxtaposition of the ordinary and extraordinary, to be found also in Auden's 'Spain', are very much in evidence in this poem. The poet points out that

> the sun shone
> As it had to on the white legs disappearing into the green
> Water . . .

Nothing, he suggests, could have been more natural. He creates the sense of the ridiculous here, too, in contrast to something that could have been so spectacular. Notice the ordinariness of the language—the ship 'had somewhere to get to', 'the dogs go on with their doggy life'. Whilst death is being meted out in an horrific way we have a view of 'the torturer's horse' rubbing itself against a tree. There is a general air of casualness which the poet attempts to convey, too, through the conversational metre that he employs. Indeed, the poem seems to open in the middle of a conversation, and Auden creates a sense of rambling even, as well as of the speaker experiencing some kind of hesitancy. This can be seen in the shape and content of the lines 'Children who did not specially want it to happen, skating/On a pond at the edge of the wood.'

It is, however, more than a commentary on the ordinary versus the spectacular in life. Auden seems to wish to examine the human condition and especially the place of 'suffering' in life. Of all the poems examined so far only one was free of this sense of pain and suffering ('Look, stranger'). The others spoke of the human lot as one of sorrow and endurance. Where peace seems evident, it is quickly threatened. Where men seem free to exercise their will there is the presence of forces which are bent on frustrating that human quality. So, too, here, even in an environment that displays the potential for beauty in man, the Musée des Beaux Arts, we find evidence of how aspiration can be effectively frustrated. Icarus stands as a symbol of man's aspiring powers. His plummeting from the heavens symbolises this element of despair in Auden's poetry.

NOTES AND GLOSSARY:

Musée des Beaux Arts: the Museum of Fine Art in Brussels, Belgium

Old Masters: great painters of the past, usually referring to any period before the nineteenth century

Brueghel: Pieter Brueghel the elder (1525−69), a Flemish painter

---

In Memory of W.B. Yeats   (44)

SUMMARY: (Part I) The opening line of Part I tells us simply when the poet died. But the stanza then goes on to show that his death was in keeping with all the many other signs of death that were apparent at the time.

The second stanza talks about the continued existence of life elsewhere, unaffected; wolves, for example, 'ran on through evergreen forests'. Like the evergreen forests, Auden suggests, Yeats's poems will never die.

The third stanza concentrates on what happened to the poet as he lay dying. Auden uses an image of revolution here to show how the various parts of his body offered their own forms of resistance, how his mind went blank, and how he gradually lost all sense and feeling. The person that was W.B. Yeats took a new form through the continued evidence of those who admired his work.

Stanza four may appear macabre in expression. What it means is that the poetry of W.B. Yeats is now expressed in many different languages. Some will treat him with respect; others will find him objectionable. The famous last two lines of this stanza mean that those who experience the poet's works will give form and meaning to what he intended.

The fifth stanza of this part repeats a sentiment that was given expression in the poem examined above, 'Musée des Beaux Arts'. Here Auden reflects on the simple fact that whilst a sad and tragic event was in progress, the process of living elsewhere continued as usual. Only some will remember it as being an unusual day.

The last stanza is of only two lines. Auden sounds melancholic and tells us that the records show that the day on which Yeats died was indeed forlorn.

(Part II) These ten lines celebrate the triumph of Yeats's poetry. Auden tells us that it will remain triumphant despite all the personal faults of Yeats himself, and all the various human factors that surrounded him in his native land. Indeed, it was the odd features of Irish society, Auden claims, that prompted him to write poetry. But Yeats's poetry never changed anything in reality. Poetry is not a force which operates beyond itself. It is satisfied to continue to live once it has been

expressed. The poet may live and die in those areas of desolate experience which inspire his words, but the words themselves move beyond
that limited environment and continue to live.

(Part III) The first stanza talks of the burial of W.B. Yeats in
romantic terms. The ground is personified as a host that welcomes
visitors. The second stanza shows that not only is the earth kind to
Yeats, but that time and history will be equally kind. Time, says
Auden, treats all merely physical forms as being of little concern. But
time respects language and all those who give it expression. It will for-
give all kinds of indiscretion in those who live by the word. Even more:
they will be honoured. The fourth stanza gives two instances of authors
who have been well treated by history. It promises that the same will
happen to Yeats.

Stanza six talks of the menaces to humanity existent at the time.
Europe is at war, nations are isolated by mutual hatred. Stanza seven
continues this sad theme and tells of the drying up of all intellectual
and emotional activity.

Stanza eight makes its appeal now to the spirit of Yeats to banish all
this darkness and show the world reasons for happiness. Stanza nine
expresses the hope that the seed his poems sow will bear rich fruit. The
poet even hopes that it may be possible to transform basically evil
things into beneficial ones. The final stanza expresses a similar wish.
Auden prays that Yeats's poems will bring solace to those who have no
hope and no reason for joy.

COMMENTARY: The poem, though in three parts, has to be considered
as a whole. Each part offers a different approach to the same topic of
W.B. Yeats's death (which occurred in January 1939), and adopts, too,
a different stylistic manner. The first part has an almost prosaic attitude
to the death of the poet. We are told factual details such as the fall of
snow, the closing of airports because of the inclement conditions, and
even the physical manner of his death. The blank-verse form that is
adopted enhances this matter-of-fact tone. However, to offset that
effect we also find more exotic references in the second stanza, namely,
to wolves in 'evergreen forests' and 'the peasant river'.

The images of revolt and rebellion that are introduced into the third
stanza do lift Yeats's death above the merely ordinary. Auden tells us
of the 'rumours' of disease and death in the poet's body; of the way the
various parts of his body—spoken of as 'provinces' and 'squares' and
'suburbs'—began to feel the ill effects. Unlike the specific statements
of the first stanza the poem now begins to sound compressed and even
obscure. We have to search for meaning in such a phrase as 'he became
his admirers'. The notion conveyed in that rather pithy statement continues in the next stanza, and is repeated in the two lines:

The words of a dead man
Are modified in the guts of the living.

The concept of artistic consistency is raised here, because we find that Auden's notion of the poet's words being affected by the active involvement of his readers and being liable to change is to some degree contrary to a later notion in Part III.

There he sees the words of the poet as being capable of more positive, active influence. Far from being changed they can bring about change. The words may be able to 'Teach the free man how to praise'.

Part I is less optimistic. Only 'a few thousand' will recall this day in January 1939. But at least this is less pessimistic than the sentiments expressed in 'Musée des Beaux Arts' where no one cared to notice the death of Icaras.

In Part II we have it boldly stated that 'poetry makes nothing happen'. This is not consistent with the view expressed in Part I where, at least, it was seen to engage the reader in some process—even if only a digestive one. It is in strong contrast, too, with the hopes held out for poetry in Part III. Auden is fond of provoking argument and response. He will do it by presenting, as in this case, some quite obviously incompatible statements. He will do it, too, by the use of quite vivid and alarming images which shock the reader into thought, as in that reference to the 'guts of the living'.

The argument in this part is largely academic and remote from real, live issues. Auden adopts the image of a remote valley and a river which is relatively untroubled. In Part III, though, he tries in the last five stanzas to relate poetry to immediate issues. War and misery create situations within which poetry can possibly work for the good. Auden hopes so. Given the serious nature of the statements in this part, the rhyming couplet form may appear inappropriate. The form is, however, suggested by that of an epitaph on a tombstone. The opening stanza is devised as just such an epitaph. But the 'poetic' suggestion that Yeats was a 'vessel' of poetry is abandoned in the next stanza. It is replaced by the macabre suggestion of decay in the statement that time is 'indifferent in a week/To a beautiful physique'. The rest of the images in the poem are not as stark and horrific as that. Rather they are vague and intangible: 'nightmare of the dark', 'seas of pity', 'bottom of the night', 'deserts of the heart'. They tend to be large, general gestures towards feeling. They lack the sense of intensely felt emotion. They indulge Auden's own 'rapture of distress'. The personification of time contributes to this lack of a sense of real commitment, to the feeling of artificiality evident in this part of the poem. With this judgement in mind it is interesting to read the following remark made by Auden to his friend Stephen Spender:

I am incapable of saying a word about Yeats because, through no fault of his, he has become for me a symbol of my own devil of authenticity, of everything which I must try to eliminate from my own poetry, false emotions, inflated rhetoric, empty sonorities.*

Part III of this poem shows plenty of evidence of those 'false emotions'.

NOTES AND GLOSSARY:

W.B. Yeats: William Butler Yeats (1865–1939), the Irish poet and dramatist
the Bourse: the French stock exchange
Kipling: Rudyard Kipling (1865–1936), the English poet and novelist
Paul Claudel: (1868–1955), the French poet, dramatist and diplomat

---

'In Praise of Limestone'   (65)

.SUMMARY: The poem opens with a statement about a basic physical property of limestone: 'it dissolves in water'. The poet suggests that this quality appeals to those who are themselves easily affected by external factors. He calls those people 'the inconstant ones'. He points out various sensuous effects of this rock formation. Visually it is pleasing with its 'rounded slopes' and aurally it appeals with the variety of liquid sounds to be experienced there. It is a place frequented by all the colourful beauties of nature. It is exactly the kind of environment to create a sense of well-being and generosity, one which creates a willingness to yield to others' wishes, just as the limestone yields to external pressures. Auden talks then about the way in which this environment provides no challenge to those who seek to 'conquer' it. It yields easily. They themselves are not driven into competition against each other— there is no great rivalry engendered between them in these surroundings. They have no 'secrets' to keep from one another. All is shared. The mountains they seek to climb do not inspire them with a sense of great danger, of defying delights. These mountains are not the kind to inspire any sense of awe; they are not like volcanoes that cannot be controlled. Those who negotiate this terrain, the poet says, do so with ease and familiarity. They have experienced no real sense of being lost in space, of being faced with the mysterious, or the inexplicable, or the frightening. If any of them falls below personal expectations then his fall is readily recognised as human and likely to happen to any of us, good or bad.

* Quoted in Charles Osborne, *W.H. Auden, The Life of a Poet*, Eyre Methuen, London, 1980, p.280.

It is a fact of nature, Auden goes on to say, that some are good and some are bad. So it is that, for different reasons, all such men do seek other environments. The good (the saints) accept the challenge offered by areas that seem to hold out no earthly fruition. They face the realities of human experience, namely that all things are transient and passing, even happiness and love, but that death is 'permanent'.

The bad, those who are looking for earthly power, go in search of another, more fruitful environment represented by the 'clays and gravels'. There, those who intended to rule and enjoy the feeling of power, will find fertile and ready soil. A third type would be seeking nothing in particular, only intent on experiencing life to the full. Such men would have no regard to the risks to be taken but would seek adventure for its own sake. They are persuaded that life is selfish and people's motives are self-centred.

The poet has to concede that there is truth in these claims. This world is not one of settled peace. There are less attractive features beneath a very thin surface. Nevertheless, there still exists within it the ability to raise questions about what is so often taken for granted by materialistic nations. A poet who speaks for such nations is himself troubled by the existence of these formations in nature shaped out of limestone. They challenge his pragmatic views of creation. Auden refers to this kind of poet as 'calling the sun, the sun'. He does not look for magic or myth. He belongs to a scientific world, a world in which answers are necessary and possible. It is a world where it is important to be ambitious, to control feelings (this is the meaning of the phrase 'the beasts who repeat themselves'), to scorn anything that is too obvious and predictable. Auden suggests that materialistic views, based on the philosophy that death is the end of everything, may well be right. Yet, he suggests, this limestone landscape offers evidence of more than that. To him it suggests different and equally valid values. It suggests the presence still of wonders and varieties. It stands for individuality. There is room for indifference to material concerns. It can represent 'a faultless love/Or the life to come'.

COMMENTARY: It is said that Auden regarded this poem as his favourite. Its theme is one that certainly dominates a great deal of his poetry. It is that of individuality. He praises individuality as expressed in this natural phenomenon. The limestone rock is unpredictable. It can take any shape. It can be unique and strange. Note the statement which he makes in what might be called the second section of the poem (beginning 'Watch, then, the band . . . '). There he talks about them walking 'Arm in arm, but never, thank God, in step'. The phrase 'in step' refers to a militaristic, marching image of uniformity. The poem, written just three years after the 1939–1945 war, readily summons up in that image the vision of jack-booted soldiers. It is an image suggested again later when he speaks of 'Indendant Caesars rose and/Left, slamming the door'. This is a deliberate echo of a statement of one of the German Nazi leaders, Joseph Goebbels (1897–1945), who declared, 'If we are defeated, we shall slam the doors of history behind us'.

The limestone environment may not be very exciting. It may not provoke feelings of awe. It may not spur man to ambition. It is undramatic. But Auden suggests that all the emotions which it fails to inspire can be taken to extremes that eventually endanger the human spirit. The most extreme statement made in this respect is that 'there is no love'. This especially would repel the romantic in Auden who likes to think of 'a faultless love'.

The poem may appear difficult. Some critics concern themselves with the location of these limestone rocks. There is a suggestion, for example, that Auden, writing as an American, is expressing his home-sickness for the cliffs of England. An alternative suggestion is that he is reflecting on the beauties of an Italian landscape. The fact is that its location does not really matter. He chooses the limestone as an analogy for what he calls being 'inconstant'. The epithet itself may appear disparaging. It is not. It simply means here that the people it represents have the free will to change and adapt—to be, in short, human. There is a personal feeling about the poem that helps to emphasise the humanity for which Auden is pleading.

Auden assumes a conversational tone addressing the reader as 'my dear' twice in the poem. The third line suggests a physical closeness between the poet and the reader whom he asks to 'Mark these rounded slopes' and 'hear these springs'. The springs themselves enhance the feeling of friendliness as they 'spurt' and 'chuckle'. Friendship is in evidence everywhere. It is there in the comradeship experienced by 'the band of rivals' who 'climb up and down . . . arm in arm'.

The poem begins to take an uglier, more unpleasant tone once the poet allows the possibility of 'bad' as well as good. We have the unat-tractive effect conjured up by references to 'a pimp' or to 'fake jewelry' or the mercenary use of great talents. The possibilities for evil are then developed through much of the latter part of the poem. There is, for example, that ugly image of those 'gamins', creatures of the gutter, who try to tempt the scientist away from lofty ideals to their own contemptible level. Their 'lively offers' could imply sexual perver-sions, or pursuit of easy money, perhaps, by a lowering of standards. The phrase 'the beasts who repeat themselves' is part of this ugliness. Auden is referring to animal instincts, of unthinking propagation.

The point of the poem, however, is that the landscape he studies symbolises the type of existence which can embrace such departures from moral standards. There is a place for the less than good, and we should be able to understand them.

The shape of Auden's poem with its long verses and sentences creates a visual effect of the landscape he is describing. It seems undisciplined. It seems to encourage a looseness without control. And yet there is a sense of an underlying control which can be demonstrated by a count of the syllables in each line. There is a pattern, which hardly varies, of thirteen syllables in one line followed by eleven in the next throughout the poem. Some degree of uniformity can thus co-exist with a sense of freedom. It is an instance of that variety of angles of perspective that, we are told at the close of the poem, is welcomed by 'the blessed'.

NOTES AND GLOSSARY:

thyme: a herb with strong-scented leaves

conduits: channels or pipes for conveying water

outcrop: rock penetrating the surface of the earth

Voluble discourse: loud conversation or argument

a good lay: a colloquial expression referring to sexual intercourse

a crater whose blazing fury ...: a volcano

nomad: a wanderer

pimp: one who lives off the earnings of prostitutes

effects that bring down the house: Auden refers to theatrical tricks of of a superficial kind calculated to appeal to an audience (the house = the audience)

Indendant Caesars: those with ambitions to rule like emperors

gamins: (*French*) street-urchins (Auden suggests that they represent those who try to interest scientists in trivial projects)

The Shield of Achilles   (71)

SUMMARY: Tha place to begin this summary is the last stanza of the poem, for the rest depends on that. The references in the last stanza are to the Greek epic *Iliad*, written about the sixth century BC. It is a story which has Achilles as its hero and tells of his exploits in the Greek war against the state of Troy. The epic was written by the Greek poet Homer.

The episode referred to in this last stanza is that in which Achilles has new armour made for him by the god Hephaestos. Thetis, named in the third line of that stanza, is the mother of Achilles. She sees that the shield that Hephaestos has made shows different scenes, some heroic, some simply horrific. Auden takes this theme and transfers it to a modern setting. The opening stanza tells us that 'she', that is the modern Thetis, looked over the shoulder of the man making the shield expecting to see a scene depicting abundance ('vines and olive trees'), stability ('well-governed cities') and security. Instead she sees a landscape that holds no promise at all, barren and colourless.

The second stanza continues this theme of a barren landscape. But what is even worse is the shield-maker's depiction of masses of people characterised by their absolute conformity and their lack of initiative.

The third stanza speaks of the influences brought to bear on the masses: the use of statistics to demonstrate truth, the flat, impersonal tones of brain-washing, the people's unquestioning submission to such persuasion and their acting like automatons.

Thetis, we are told, looked into the shield for evidence of heroism, of devotion and meaningful sacrifice. But, as the fifth stanza tells us, she saw instead an act of sacrifice that had no sense of glory about it. Those responsible for it seemed indifferent. The location and atmosphere were both equally uninspiring. The crowd that watched the ritual execution were passive and uninvolved. Those who were executed are depicted as completely helpless and insignificant. They could not hope for any help in a world where power lay beyond their control. They had lost all self-respect and their deaths were as trivial as that of any other man before them. The seventh stanza tells us that Thetis then looked into the shield for evidence of human achievement and grace and joy. Instead all she saw was a field that had never seen cultivation or fruitfulness. The eighth stanza shows a picture of an abandoned child who has gone wild and knows only the law of the wild. He knows murder and violence. He knows no pity. He has never experienced truth. The final stanza tells us of the distress Thetis suffered at what had been created to please Achilles. He was the hero who was renowned for his courage and prowess in battle.

COMMENTARY: In the original story the scenes depicted on the shield would have been heroic. Here Auden has adopted an anti-heroic stance. He has shown civilisation as he so often sees it. His mention of the influence of statistics and their being used to demonstrate some truth may remind you of another poem in this collection. 'The Unknown Citizen' (number 46) shows the function of 'the Bureau of Statistics'.

Notice how in that poem a 'Marble Monument is Erected by the State' in honour of this citizen. This phrase provides an ironic contrast to the 'Marble well-governed cities' mentioned in 'The Shield of Achilles'. In the latter case, the marble represents a sense of grandeur; in the first case the marble represents the impersonal treatment of life and death in the modern state. In 'The Shield of Achilles' Auden stresses this notion of the depersonalisation of the human being. The phrase 'a million boots in line' sums up the uniformity and conformity that, to Auden, meant the death of the spirit. It is possible that the 'boots' here signify a military conflict, too, and Auden despairs of all that modern warfare means. The 'million' indicates the massive scale of war, and the whole stanza in which this occurs suggests the use of human beings as brain-washed victims. The same theme is repeated in stanza three.

The notion of sacrifice in the poem seems to point towards the act of sacrifice central to Christianity. The 'three pale figures' referred to may be those of Christ and the two thieves crucified with him. Christ saw his sacrifices as universally significant. Christians, in consequence, are expected to view it in the same light. They, too, would see it as a significant contribution to civilisation. Auden questions here the validity of any such views of this sacrifice, given our modern experience of the world. It is a world that offers no sense of joy or grandeur or worth. The only men with any sense of importance are those whom Auden obviously despises. This is suggested, for example, in the three lines that begin the sixth stanza:

The mass and majesty of this world, all
That carries weight and always weighs the same,
Lay in the hands of others.

The choice of such words as 'mass and majesty' creates a sense of importance and weightiness. The concepts themselves are suggestive of something significant, and the simple use of alliterative repetition adds to a sense of impressiveness. The lines, too, have a sweeping effect which helps to 'carry' the weight.

Other than that brief burst of rhetoric, though, the language and structure of the verse do not assist any suggestion of importance. Indeed where there is hope expressed of just such an effect it is quickly dashed. That is the function of those three stanzas which speak of Thetis looking into the shield in the hope of seeing something of value. In each case hope is built up and then shattered. The three stanzas in question, namely, the first, fourth and seventh, have a choral effect. Notice how they all open with the same line and build up the notion of promise which is then destroyed by the recurring words 'but there'. These three stanzas are distinguished from the others by a change in rhythm and rhyme. Indeed, they have a rhythm which hints at the unreal, whilst the more prosaic rhythm of the other stanzas suggests an all-too-real reality. These latter stanzas, in their turn, have a regular rhyming pattern which itself suggests the artificiality of the new vision of the world. It suggests a sense of contrivance even in a world that boasts of being hard and unimaginative. So, for example, in the fifth stanza we have the crass indifference of the officials at the execution conveyed in the telling of the joke. The joke is told as an 'aside' which is conveyed as such in Auden's poem by being placed in brackets. It is all very appropriate, and it is a delight to see the artist at work. At the same time, it could be argued that the word 'joke' was introduced because of the need for a word to rhyme with 'folk' in the fourth line and 'spoke' in the fifth. Auden's work can thus be seen as either brilliantly inspired or merely functional—or both. Perhaps those who admire the modern as contrasted with the Classical world would argue that it, too, is a strange mixture of both the inspired and the functional. Auden probably deliberately sets out to create exactly that kind of doubt and ambivalence.

NOTES AND GLOSSARY:

Achilles: a Greek hero who took part in the Graeco-Trojan war

Libation: an offering of drink to the gods in sacrificial ceremonies

an arbitrary spot: a location chosen for no particular reason

---

'Horae Canonicae' (75:I Prime)

The general title of the poem refers, in Latin, to the canonical hours. These are the hours of prayer. The first or 'prime' hour is at six o'clock, the third or 'terce' hour is at nine o'clock, the 'sext' or sixth is at noon, 'nones' at three o'clock, 'vespers' in the evening, 'compline' the last prayer of the day, and 'lauds' the first morning prayer. Monks were obliged to chant their prayers at these specified times.

Auden speaks of his own waking moments. He can see himself then as a person distinct from his body. In the last line of the first stanza of 'Prime' he speaks of experiencing an existence 'between my body and the day'. The awakening is seen as quite dramatic. It is a flinging open and shutting of gates: an opening on to a new day and a shutting off of the experiences of the night. These are seen as characterised by rebellion. They are unattractive ('ill-favoured'), badly disposed to others ('ill-natured') and something to be disowned ('disenfranchised, widowed, and orphaned'). He feels as though he is taking on a fresh identity with the coming of the day. It is almost like an entirely new creation—as though he has been walking amongst the dead and now becomes a feeling being.

The second stanza, beginning 'Holy this moment' provides a hint of how the poet is enjoying the experience of re-creating this time of re-creation. There is a deliberate pun involved in the use of 'holy' and 'wholly' and the phrasing echoes the 'laconic' nature of the awakening of day. The poet talks about 'the light's laconic outcry' by which he suggests the brief and instant announcement of the coming of daylight. The immediacy of the experience is boldly caught in the references to the things that immediately face him in his bedroom environment—the bed—the sheet and the wall. There is, too, that light-hearted way of showing how the body gradually comes alive. His arm, for example, is not yet recognised as belonging to him. It has still to awake and be recognised by his mind. The will is one part of the mind. Memory is another. Auden says that memory's first function is to remember him himself, to recall even his name.

Whilst his memory and will are still experiencing this process of re-creation Auden likes to reflect that at that time he is completely inno-cent. For, to have sin, one must act with intention and full understand-ing of the evil involved, and at this moment of waking none of these faculties are in operation. The act of breathing, of giving expression to life, is an exercise of his will. It proves that he wants knowledge, that he wishes to be an identifiable person, that he even wants to die. Those external proofs of life that he can see, like 'the flat roofs of the fishing village' are not yet real to him. He cannot yet summon up happy mem-ories of his experiences there. All they are, it seems, are external means he will use to bring about his own personal fate. His own body is seen in the same way. Even a thing as personal to himself as his name, his iden-tity, is viewed as just another piece of evidence of his responsibility in life.

The last four lines of 'Prime' show us that the waking moments are a picture in brief of the historical context in which he lives. Those mom-ents are not insignificant. They demonstrate the links between such an everyday unfolding of life and the continuous development of historical certainty.

COMMENTARY: For a complete understanding of this one poem it has to be seen in the context of the whole of the 'Horae Canonicae'. From ref-erences within the other poems we deduce that the 'typical' day Auden is describing is, in fact, Good Friday, the Christian feast which celeb-rates the crucifixion of Christ. It is an historic event referred to in the commentary on 'The Shield of Achilles' (p.30). In 'Terce' Auden says that the 'victim' will know 'by sundown/We shall have had a good Friday'. In 'Sext' he concludes his poem with the lines:

> to worship
> The Prince of this world like us,
>
> at this noon, on this hill,
> in the occasion of this dying.

The 'hill' in this instance is that of Golgotha or Calvary where Christ was crucified. In 'Prime' Auden is talking about the historical back-ground to that act of sacrifice. It was necessary because of the existence of sin. Sin, according to orthodox Christianity, came into being by an act of sinful disobedience on the part of Adam. At that point Paradise was lost. And we notice the reference to this in the poem. With that action, it is said, death became part of nature. The 'flesh' that was given as a gift to man is now a means by which he will bring about his own destruction. The religious impulse in the poem is thus everywhere in evidence. It may be that the Christian emphasis is too emphatic, too didactic for many people's tastes. But Auden wrote a great many poems with this kind of emphasis after his conversion to Christian belief. The poem can be read and enjoyed without this specific religious reference although it does lose a great deal once denied that significance. The gradual re-awakening of the man is delightfully portrayed with more than a suggestion of good humour. Auden spoke of the fun he had in composing the verse, especially in devising the variety of rhyme within the poem. You will see that he has not relied on end-rhymes but rhymes within lines. This can often affect the ordering of lines to the extent that we may lose the various connections. In one instance this searching for the rhyme dramatically catches the sense of possibility of loss: thus, in these lines from the third stanza Auden offers us the word 'cost' and then almost hides its rhyming partner:

> To be different, to die and the cost,
>   No matter how, is Paradise
> Lost . . .

He introduces his literary reference to Milton's *Paradise Lost* in an impudent kind of way, almost daring us to find it. And, of course, if we do not find it then it *is* 'lost'. It is an audacity of style which appears also in the pun referred to in the summary of the poem during our examination of the stanza (see p.31). The poem was subjected to a great deal of revision in which Auden set out to introduce these rhyming effects. He claimed that this attention to verbal felicities helped make his meanings more specific and, at the same time, stimulated thought. In the opening stanza we find references to rebellious movements (a 'fronde' means 'violent political opposition'). Originally he had written that the rebellion would be 'shut off'. His revised version was, as you can see, 'Quell'. This is not only more appropriate when speaking of putting down a rebellion, but also provides a rhyme with the first part of his word 'rebellious'. This was in turn, substituted for the original descriptive word 'angry'. Auden's virtuosity is displayed in the variety of verse-forms he adopts throughout the seven parts that make up this poem.

NOTES AND GLOSSARY:

'*Immolatus vincerit*': (*Latin*) 'Being lifted up, he will conquer.' The Latin is taken from one of the prayers of the Church for Good Friday. 'Immolatus' in Classical as opposed to Church Latin can mean being slain, sacrificed

rummage:	searching
fronde:	violent opposition (in politics)
Disenfranchised:	having lost the freedom
laconic:	brief
Adam:	the name given to the first man
Paradise Lost:	the epic poem of twelve books written by John Milton (1608–74)

Part 3

Commentary

IN PART 2 IT HAS BEEN THE INTENTION to make Auden's poetry both accessible and comprehensible, to demonstrate that meaning is possible. This may seem an extraordinary thing to say, but much criticism of Auden does suggest that his hallmark is that of obscurity rather than clarity. By discussing specific poems in Part 2, it is possible not only to show the meaning but also to prove that such meaning is accessible.

In this part of the book, references will be made to those poems already studied, but there will also be wide-ranging references to other poems in *Selected Poems*. The student should read all of these poems (and those parts which are not poetry, such as 'Caliban to the Audience') in order to try to gain the full 'flavour' of Auden. The various sections of this part of the book will demonstrate the diversity of Auden's verse, language, symbolism and imagery.

Themes

Individuality

One pressing theme in Auden's poetry is the need to preserve individual identity. Modern living, particularly the pressures of bureaucracy, poses a threat to this sense of identity. In an early poem, 'It is time for the destruction of error' (8:IV, in *Selected Poems*), he talks of the attacks that are planned against the individual. He tells us that plans are being made:

> To censor the play of the mind, to enforce
> Conformity.

This is an Early Warning—the poem was written in 1929—that is reiterated in other forms in later poems. Thus, for example, ten years later in one of his poems, 'In Memory of W.B. Yeats' (44), he utters a prayer for the freedom of the individual not only threatened but actually imprisoned:

> In the deserts of the heart
> Let the healing fountain start,
> In the prison of his days
> Teach the free man how to praise.

Auden sees this as the function of the poet. It is the poet who can help bring this kind of solace and relief. But, in a poem published in the same volume as 'In Memory of W.B. Yeats', he speaks of the identity of the individual as having already been destroyed. He is merely a number, part of what we might now call 'a computer print-out'. Notice how 'The Unknown Citizen' (46) is dedicated to someone identified only by his number: 'To JS/07/M/378'. This ironic touch makes Auden's bitter point in a succinct manner. The poem goes on to identify the citizen as a faceless creation of the 'Bureau of Statistics', 'One against whom there was no official complaint'.

In the poem which follows it in the set text, 'September, 1939', Auden talks of the oppression 'obsessing our private lives'. It is a grim and frightening picture that he creates, sitting, as he says, 'In one of the dives/On Fifty-Second Street'. He tells us that each man and each woman expects to be recognised as an individual. That is what he means when he says:

> For the error bred in the bone
> Of each woman and each man
> Craves what it cannot have,
> Not universal love
> But to be loved alone.

Such statements about this matter of individualism and the need for it are very specific. Auden's alarm at the threats to the individual and the freedom to choose have prompted him to express himself in almost a blunt manner.

In 'In Praise of Limestone' (65) we find him approaching the problem rather more obliquely—and, some would suggest, 'obscurely'. The theme of individuality is presented here as an appeal for the freedom to express one's emotions freely, to be free to change at will. Auden draws an analogy with the rock whose beauty is in its ability to adapt itself to changing conditions. It is not cast into a rigid, uniform mould. His closing lines in this poem create an idyll, an ideal environment for the human being to live in:

> but when I try to imagine a faultless love
> Or the life to come, what I hear is the murmur
> Of underground streams, what I see is a limestone landscape.

Contrast this sense of freedom for the individual with that provided, say, in a poem written four years later: 'The Shield of Achilles' (71). We are told in the allegory that the mother of Achilles looked into the shield that was made for her son. She expected exactly such an idyllic landscape as that which is suggested in those closing lines of 'In Praise of Limestone':

>   She looked over his shoulder
>   For vines and olive trees,
>   Marble well-governed cities,
>   And ships upon untamed seas*

Instead, he tells us, the mother saw a vision of automatons, of those who had been brain-washed, who had lost all sense of identity.

In his poem 'Prologue at Sixty' (90), Auden sums up his esteem for individuality in two lines:

>   a Mind of Honor must acknowledge
>   the happy eachness of all things

The role of the poet

In 'Prologue at Sixty' Auden asked whether what he had to say meant anything to anybody else. The lines that follow have a particular relevance, perhaps, to your present endeavours as a student. They ought not, however, be seen to be applicable only to that specific situation:

>   Can Sixty make sense to Sixteen-Plus?
>   What has my camp in common with theirs,
>   with buttons and beards and Be-Ins†?
>   Much, I hope.

This had always been his hope. He saw the role of the poet as a public one. The poet had a public voice. He believed that the poet had a message to convey. This is cogently expressed in part of 'Caliban to the Audience' (see *Selected Poems*, p.171).

> Having learnt his language, I begin to feel something of the serio-comic embarrassment of the dedicated dramatist, who, in representing to you your condition of estrangement from the truth, is doomed to fail the more he succeeds, for the more truthfully he paints the condition, the less clearly can he indicate the truth from which it is estranged, the brighter his revelation of the truth in its order, its justice, its joy, the fainter shows his picture of your actual condition . . . and, ultimately, what other aim and justification has he, what else exactly *is* the artistic gift which he is forbidden to hide, if not to make you unforgettably conscious of the ungarnished offended gap between what you so questionably are and what you are commanded without any question to become . . . ?

---

* Notice how that last image, of the 'untamed seas', indicates Auden's concern for the exercise of freedom.
† This is a reference to phenomena occurring at the time (1967), such as 'Sit-Ins' and 'Love-Ins', which were forms of communal or group solidarity.

There is a great sense of irony in giving Caliban these words. He was the monster in Shakespeare's late play *The Tempest*. In that play the magician Prospero had tried to teach him a new culture, had tried to bridge that 'gap' in Caliban's development – and failed! Here Auden has Caliban instructing the audience about their own ignorance, and the efforts of the dramatist. The dramatist, in this instance, represents any poet or artist.

One poem in our *Selected Poems* that can be seen to demonstrate Auden's view of the artist or the poet is 'Musée des Beaux Arts'. He makes his view clear in the opening two lines:

> About suffering they were never wrong,
> The Old Masters: how well they understood
> Its human position.

Thus he shows us the insights of the artist. He instances how the painter Brueghel has captured the human condition so appositely in one of his works, 'Icarus'. One point Auden seems anxious to make here is that the common man is insensitive. He is preoccupied with his material concerns: he either never lifts his eyes to heaven, or having done so, chooses to ignore the message he receives. The painter, he feels has captured this lack of sensibility perfectly, and, in accordance with his public duty, has given it due expression.

Despite the sense of assurance apparent in this poem, there is another, published in the same volume of poems as 'Musée des Beaux Arts' (*Another Time*, 1940), which is not so confident about the role of the poet in regard to the public. 'In Memory of W.B. Yeats' actually states that 'poetry makes nothing happen'. This seems a supreme expression of pessimism. Yet, despite all this, Auden is to assert later in the same poem that the poet has to persevere in his efforts to instruct and lift the human spirit despite such a sense of despair:

> Follow, poet, follow right
> To the bottom of the night,
> With your unconstraining voice
> Still persuade us to rejoice.

We do, however, find in his poetry other expressions of disquiet about the true effectiveness of the poet. In 'The Waters', part of the work called 'The Quest' (52) he links the 'Poet, oracle and wit' and speaks of them all as 'unsuccessful anglers' who are unable to achieve their aims. Nevertheless, the poet feels he must persevere. At the end of his poem 'Oxford' (39) it may be the poet to whom he is referring when he speaks of:

> The low unflattering voice
> That rests not till it find a hearing.

To return, finally, to the reference to Caliban earlier in this section (p.37). The extract there is taken from Auden's 'Commentary on Shakespeare's *The Tempest*,' whose main title is *The Sea and the Mirror*. The magician Prospero failed with his creature Caliban; the failure of such magic is significant in the present context, for Auden did not see poetry as magic but as a kind of mirror. He put it this way:

> Art ... is not Magic, i.e. a means by which the artist communicates or arouses his feelings in others, but a mirror in which they become conscious of what their own feelings really are ... *

The spiritual versus the material

Auden opens one of his poems, 'Ode to Terminus' (92), with the lines:

> The High Priests of telescopes and cyclotrons
> keep making pronouncements about happenings ...

The ironic juxtaposition of the term 'High Priest' and these scientific references sums up succinctly the conflict between the scientific materialism that dominates the world of his later years and the spiritual realities he embraces. Trained as a scientist, he yet decries what he calls 'our colossal immodesty' which 'has plundered and poisoned' our world. He prays to God

> By whose grace, also, every gathering
> of two or three in confident amity
>   repeats the pentecostal marvel,
>   as each in each finds his right translator.

His references here are, firstly, to Christ's statement (in the Bible, Matthew 18.20) that where two or three are gathered in his name, he, too, will be present; and, secondly, to the event at the Feast of Pentecost when, according to Scripture (Acts 2: 1–2), the Spirit of God came down on men. Auden's confident integration of such scriptural references into his poetry demonstrates his commitment to religion. Even great achievements in science and technology, as recorded 'Moon Landing' (95), only prompt him to scorn science which, he says, ruins our civilisation! He just expresses the hope that higher spiritual notions will serve to make our existence at least tolerable:

> Our apparatniks will continue making
> the usual squalid mess called History:
>   all we can pray for is that artists,
>   chefs and saints may still appear to blithe it.

* In a review of T.S. Eliot's *A Choice of Kipling's Verse*, in *The New Republic*, 1943.

In 'Talking to Myself' (97) he rebukes Science for thinking of the creation of the individual as 'A random event'. Instead, he sees it as 'A true miracle,' and, of course, given our awareness of his concern for individualism, it is natural that he should defend the notion of such a deliberate act of creation. Auden's landscape paintings often highlight this invasion of science and the manner in which it mars our existence. Thus, he will take, say, the traditional theme of the river finding its way through a devastated landscape. Everywhere it touches is characterised by industrial or technological rivalry and by an almost inevitable sense of degradation:

> Polluted, bridged by girders, banked by concrete,
> now it bisects a polyglot metropolis,
> ticker-tape, taxi, brothel, foot-lights country,
> *à la mode* always.

'River Profile' (89)

This poem was written in 1966, but Auden's appreciation of spiritual realities can be traced back much further than that. He tells of an intellectual and emotional conversion to Christianity before the outbreak of the Second World War:

> I met an Anglican layman, and for the first time in my life felt myself in the presence of personal sanctity ... I felt transformed into a person who was incapable of doing or thinking anything base or unloving.*

And his friend, Stephen Spender, writes:

> When, early in 1950, Auden together with other intellectuals answered a questionnaire about his religious beliefs, he alone of all those who answered seemed to experience no difficulty in accepting the strictest dogmas of the Christian faith.†

It was at about that time that Auden wrote his 'Horae Canonicae' which takes its name from the prayers of the Christian church. Its various parts are named after the hours at which those prayers are to be said. In 'Vespers'—the evening prayer—we find this conflict of the spiritual versus the material represented in almost every stanza, or section. For example Auden contrasts what he calls his Eden, that is, his vision of paradise, with a New Jerusalem imagined by what he calls his 'Anti-type'. The New Jerusalem represents a materialistic view of things. Thus, he tells us:

---

* *Modern Canterbury Pilgrims*, ed. J.A. Pike, A.R. Mowbray, Oxford, 1946, p.41.
† Stephen Spender, *World within World*, Hamish Hamilton, London, 1951, p.56.

· In my Eden we have a few beam-engines, saddle-tank locomotives,
overshot waterwheels, and other beautiful pieces of obsolete
machinery to play with: In his New Jerusalem even chefs will be
cucumber-cool machine minders.

Auden saw 'chefs' as one of the artists of our world; to become
'machine-minders' would be one of the most degrading forms of work.
The only good machine for him, it would seem from this, is a dead
('obsolete') machine. In another part of the poem he says that 'In his
New Jerusalem the temples will be empty'.

Auden's language

Despite Auden's concern for the spiritual and his fear of the advance of
materialism, his language is very much of a down-to-earth nature.
Look, for example, at 'The Summer holds: upon its glittering lake'
(24). Here he introduces once more a sense of conflict between spiritual
and material values. In order to emphasise the existence and
pervasiveness of the latter he brings into his poem specific references to
trade names and prosaic terms like 'filling stations'.

> Tourists to whom the Tudor cafés
> Offer Bovril and buns upon Breton ware
> With leather-work as a sideline; Filling stations
> Supplying petrol from rustic pumps.

Notice here the colloquial phrase 'as a sideline'. Auden likes to
introduce such terms to indicate the very mundanity of much that
passes for a full life, because he is very concerned about the
unsatisfactory nature of merely material existence. He is anxious about
the lack of aspiration and fulfilment in such modern living. This
anxiety sometimes finds expression in language which appears flippant
and trivial. Auden deliberately employs such language to stress the
insignificance of many lives. *Selected Poems* contains one outstanding
example of this use of language. It is 'Miss Gee' (36). This poem
describes the meaningless life of a spinster whose only claim to fame
lies eventually in her death. She is quite insignificant in appearance:

> She'd a slight squint in her left eye,
>   Her lips they were thin and small,
> She had narrow sloping shoulders
>   And she had no bust at all.

She had no taste in colours:

> She'd a purple mac for wet days
>   A green umbrella too to take.

Yet, after her death, it is discovered that she provided considerable medical interest:

> We seldom see a sarcoma
>   As far advanced as this.

We are often reminded of Auden's scientific background and the presence of the word 'sarcoma' here (it means a tumour) serves to exemplify his fondness for introducing such exact terminology into the language in his poems.

This is not the only example of his light verse in *Selected Poems*. We have 'O what is that sound which so thrills the ear' (18) and two other ballads: 'Lady, weeping at the crossroads' (50) and 'The Willow-Wren and the Stare' (72). In this last poem we find again a fine example of Auden's delight in shocking by his language:

> Forgive these loves that dwell in me,
>   These brats of greed and fear,
> The honking bottom-pinching clown,
>   The snivelling sonneteer.

We may begin to think that Auden has an obsession with 'bottoms'. For in that magnificent poem 'Musée des Beaux Arts' (42) Auden seeks again to show his irreverence and perhaps to shock. For, in talking of the achievements of 'The Old Masters' he talks of the way they, too, were ready to introduce the common touch, of how they would be quite ready to depict a horse as it 'scratches its innocent behind on a tree'. In his own portrait of 'The Unknown Citizen' (46) he offers us a satiety, an overwhelming abundance of such ordinary terms and language. He does this in order to spell out the lack of colour in everyday life:

> And our Social Psychology workers found
> That he was popular with his mates and liked a drink.
> The Press are convinced that he bought a paper every day
> And that his reactions to advertisements was normal in every way.

Auden is often accused of obscurity, and though the language examined so far could not be charged with that, there are occasions when obscurity threatens to descend. In many poems he shows a fondness for polysyllabic words, or, better still polysyllabic phrases which are, presumably, there to add a sense of importance and of occasion. One such phrase, from 'In Sickness and in Health' (54), neatly sums up the effect of such tricks of language—they threaten to lead to merely 'glittering generalities'.

His great friend and collaborator, Christopher Isherwood, spoke of Auden's lack of concern with language in his early poetry in these terms:

If I liked one line, he would keep it and work it into a new poem. In this way, whole poems were constructed which were simply antho-logies of my favourite lines, entirely regardless of grammar or sense. This is the simple explanation of much of Auden's celebrated obscurity.*

This sounds alarming and perhaps somewhat exaggerated. There are no obvious examples of this technique being employed in any of the poems in the present selection. There are, however, many instances of abbreviated expressions of meaning. Auden is, for example, fond of omitting the definite or indefinite article, or of linking words: look, for example, at these lines from Part I of 'It was Easter as I walked in the public gardens' (8):

> Where solitary man sat weeping on a bench,
> Hanging his head down, with his mouth distorted
> Helpless and ugly as an embryo chicken.

The omission of 'a' before 'solitary', and of the word 'as' before 'distorted' does interfere with the cohesion of this sentence. It is not a serious interference in this short extract, but its cumulative effect in a poem does make reading more difficult. Thus, for example, in Part II of the same poem (8) we have these lines:

> Coming out of me living is always thinking,
> Thinking changing and changing living,
> Am feeling as it was seeing—

Something is missing here, for there is no obvious subject for the verb 'Am'. The language, or use of language, creates a disjointed and disturbing effect.

Symbols

The landscape

This is one of Auden's favourite symbols. He often invites us to look at a landscape and draw our conclusions. In the poem 'The Summer holds: upon its glittering lake' (24) he presents the landscape quite dramatically: 'There it stands amidst your darling scenery.' But then he asks the reader what this 'darling scenery' means to him and what he actually sees. 'Man,' he says, 'is changed by his living'. The evidence is that this living leads to decay and neglect of the spirit:

---

* 'Some Notes on Auden's Early Poetry', *New Verse* (Auden Double Number), November 1937, p.4.

I see beams falling, fences broken,
Pasture not ploughland, weeds not wheat.

This is a picture of abandonment which mirrors that created in the opening poem in this selection, 'Who stands, the crux left of the watershed.' (1). The opening passage in that poem describes a scene of desolation, of 'an industry already comatose', of neglected and abandoned machinery. The 'stranger' who may happen to call here is encouraged to move away for 'This land, cut off, will not communicate'. There is, in contrast, an invitation to another stranger, in another poem, to stand and absorb the lessons of another, more idyllic, landscape. In the poem 'Look, stranger, at this island now' (27) Auden invites the stranger to give full range to his senses and revel in the environment; he invites him to listen to the assuring sounds of nature:

And silent be,
That through the channels of the ear
May wander like a river
The swaying sound of the sea.

The scene could stand for itself, but it is fruitful, too, to see the landscape as symbolising a rich, inner life. This is obviously the function of such a landscape as that presented in the poem 'In Praise of Limestone' (65). The last three lines of the poem point to the symbolic meaning of the poem which needs to be read in their light.

In contrast to these natural landscapes and the good they represent in the life of man is that other familiar landscape in Auden's poetry, of the City. This is seen to be in conflict with the aims of nature and the natural landscape. Auden represents it in his poem 'Memorial for a City' (68) as the source of all men's ills and distress. In one stanza, he shows how nature was put on trial by those who spoke for the City and confessed to having 'no soul'. Meanwhile he seeks to demonstrate that all the evils of man were perpetrated in the environs of a city. Notice the irony of Auden's epigraph to this poem in which he quotes from the work of a medieval mystic, Juliana of Norwich. She uses the City as a symbol in a way that is exactly opposite to Auden's use of it, since she speaks of it as divine, calling it 'the City of God'. For Auden it symbolises all that opposes God.

War

The conflict between nature and the City obvious in the symbolic landscapes of Auden's poetry also provides us with another pervasive symbol in his poems. Man's life is seen as a warfare and images from that experience proliferate in his poetry. Thus in poem Number 3 we have references to spies and saboteurs; in poem IV of Number 8 we hear 'It is time for the destruction of error'; and in his poem 'Oxford' (39) we are told that 'all the glittering prizes' are promised 'to the sharp sword'.

One of the most developed examples of this symbol is to be found in the poem 'The Shield of Achilles' (71). Here, in the related symbol of the shield, Auden presents us with the contrasting perspectives of a civilisation that is flourishing and one that is in disarray:

> She looked over his shoulder
>   For vines and olive trees,
> Marble well-governed cities,
>   And ships upon untamed seas,
> But there on the shining metal
>   His hands had put instead,
> An artificial wilderness
>   And a sky like lead.

Notice again the intrusion of a landscape effect in those last two lines. The symbols of conflict and landscape are often similarly juxtaposed. When in later poems Auden moves into the areas of psychology he often demonstrates the sense of conflict within the individual by this very device of representing a landscape. As he says in his 'Bucolics' (74), VI, 'Plains', when speaking of the variety of frustrations and disillusionment he has suffered in life:

> As it is, though, I know them personally
> Only as a landscape common to two nightmares.

The journey

It is a truism to think of life as a journey. Yet, despite the obvious dangers involved in using platitudes, this is a symbol that Auden demonstrably enjoys employing. A series of poems entitled 'The Quest' (52) reveals the early, unsteady steps of the traveller as he sets out to discover his life's meaning, followed by descriptions of the obstacles and hindrances that lie in his way until, in 'The Garden', he finds 'All journeys die here'. This is a theme which is to be found in poems written much earlier. Thus, in poem 8, Part III, he describes the life of a man as an attempt at self-discovery, a journey which too often ends in frustration. But it is one that has to be undertaken in the hope that it will lead to fruition. It is a carefully developed example of this symbol. Auden talks first of the initial hopes experienced on our journey through life. We begin with high hopes. We believe that what we learn to love will last. This almost always leads to frustration. It is then that we begin the more demanding phase in our lives. We resemble, he says, foreign travellers discovering new lands. They have to work hard to find themselves, to settle in, and to make their journey worthwhile. In much the same way, says the poet, the individual must find his true identity and learn what it is to be happy. In his poem 'Since you are going to begin today' (9), Auden repeats this notion of a search for fulfilment. He is not as optimistic as before, and warns that

> Before you reach the frontier you are caught;
> Others have tried it and will try again

Notice here how the symbol of conflict begins to re-present itself. The symbol of the journey, of the quest and search, is intimately linked with that of a hero, and in his poem 'In Time of War' (40), Part XXI, we find Auden applauding the fact that this searching and this heroism will continue because, too often, the hope of success is thwarted and destroyed:

> The life of man is never quite completed;
> The daring and the chatter will go on:
> But, as an artist feels his power gone,
> These walk the earth and know themselves defeated.

What Auden eventually concludes in his symbol of the Quest is that, too often, we use such a journey for its own sake. We use it as a means of personal self-discovery, not of finding out about others. We use it as a mark of achievement in itself. In that case, he claims, the journey has been wasted.

This point of view is most dramatically presented in one of his later poems, 'Moon Landing' (95), written in 1969. He sees it as 'A grand gesture', as the natural fruition of all those searchings and investigations that began when 'the first flint was flaked'—that is, when science was born and scientists began searching for the truth. But, despite the achievement, the journey was in vain if, as he says, 'our selves . . . still don't fit us exactly'.

Auden's imagery

Auden is not often seen as a nature poet. We find very few poems that present us with simple descriptions of nature for its own sake. Nature and its landscapes are often used to indicate something else in Auden's thinking. There are occasional exceptions to this and one of the most outstanding is certainly found in *Selected Poems*: 'Look, stranger, at this island now'. Auden's images there are buoyant and optimistic. He is revelling in the sights and sounds of nature:

And the shingle scrambles after the sucking surf, and the gull lodges
A moment on its sheer side.

The scene is alive and moving. Simple delight is everywhere evident in
the imagery.

Contrast this use of natural imagery with other uses. In 'Look stranger' Auden is able to create an idyllic scene through the water-imagery
which is part of the picture. In 'Out of the lawn I lie in bed' (20) we see him
using images from the same source to create quite a different effect:

Soon through the dykes of our content
The crumpling flood will force a rent,
    And, taller than a tree,
Hold sudden death before our eyes
Whose river-dreams long hid the size
And vigours of the sea.

In that last line we see again his fascination with the power of the sea,
but it is in contrast with the idyll it represented in the other poem. Now
it is potentially destructive. We see the same image of destruction
through water in the opening two lines of that stanza also.

Later, in the same poem, Auden talks of how the waters will 'retreat'.
Thus the images of war and violence already begin to appear in his
poetry. In his poem 'September 1, 1939' (47) he uses the image of attack
to describe his own position. He says he is 'Beleaguered by the same/
Negation and despair' as the rest of creation. In many of his poems he
employs the imagery of sleep and dreams and, even there, images of
threat and war penetrate. In 'Memorial for a City' (68) occur the
remarkable lines: 'Across our sleep/The barbed wire also runs'.

The barbed wire can be an image of protection—it keeps out the
enemy. It is, however, more likely to be an image of oppression. It pre-
vents liberty and freedom of movement. It is an image which occurs
again, for example, in 'The Shield of Achilles' where 'Barbed wire
enclosed an arbitrary spot', where people awaited a barbaric execution.

Auden's imagery is often used to create just this effect of horror and
repulsion. His nature imagery, so beautiful in a poem like 'Look, stranger', often becomes identified with war and horror. This association has
already been noted in earlier poems. He continues to link the two, and in
'River Profile' (89) the traditional idyllic picture of the river's journey is
satirised. The river is seen to cross territory that is characterised by all
that is unattractive until the river, as he says, 'wearies to its final/act of
surrender.' The territory it travels through is an industrialised landscape,
and much of Auden's imagery throughout his poems is derived from
industrialisation. He sees the machine as something that has made the

'squalid mess called History' ('Moon Landing', 95). One dramatic example of this destructive incursion of the machine into our lives is provided in his poem 'In Time of War' (40). There he talks of the 'engines' which 'bear them through the sky'. Those who fly those aeroplanes are blinded to the destructive nature of what they are doing. The aeroplane is not just an aeroplane: it represents all that stands for death and disaster in our lives.

In his poem on the 'Moon Landing' Auden says he wants to resist the realities discovered by man and still think of the moon as he did when a child. This is an idea that he used, too, when talking of the sun in his 'Ode to Terminus' (92). There he says he would rather think of the sunshine as 'a friendly/presence not a photonic bombardment'. In other words, Auden wishes he could always belong to the idyll of 'Look stranger': he would like to have been a nature poet. In his poem 'A Thanksgiving' (99) he claims that 'Nature allures me' but that is something that is not so very much in evidence in the images of war, threat and devastation that pervade so much of his poetry in *Selected Poems*. Like his river in 'River Profile' Nature 'puts off majesty'.

Auden's versification

Auden is reported to have said 'I always have two things in my head—I always have a theme and the form. The form looks for the theme, the theme looks for the form, and when they come together you're able to write'. We have already looked at some key themes in evidence in the poems in this selection. The forms in which they are expressed suggest more than the one-to-one relationship claimed by Auden. The fascination that questions of technique held for him is, according to one critic, 'Auden's chief danger'.*

Another serious criticism of Auden is that his verse tends towards obscurity, and it has already been noted that one cause for such obscurity is to be found in relatively significant omissions of single words. His versification, however, often presents a challenge to the reader, a challenge to be met. There is a danger that Auden wishes to pose as a sage, and so the more problematic his expression of ideas, the wiser he hopes to sound. So, for example, we have the stanza from a poem already partly used to illustrate his compressed style:

> Coming out of me living is always thinking,
> Thinking changing and changing living,
> Am feeling as it was seeing—
> In city leaning on harbour parapet
> To watch a colony of duck below . . .

* John Bayley, *The Romantic Survival: A Study in Poetic Evolution*, Constable, London, 1957, p.131.

> Shadow know not of homesick foreigner
> Nor restlessness of intercepted growth.

The meaning *can* be unravelled; but the poet *has* made it difficult. In his 'Epitaph on a Tyrant' (43), Auden said that one characteristic of the man had been that 'the poetry he invented was easy to understand'. In such a case, it needed no application of thought or intellect, it never exercised the imagination. It might have the bland persuasiveness, for example, of a television advertisement. Auden would not wish for that, for, as he once said, 'if language is corrupted, thought is corrupted'.

One way in which Auden commands our attention is in his employment of what has been called 'the long verse-sentences'. This is well illustrated in his own favourite poem 'In Praise of Limestone' (65). In this poem his image is of water which eats into the landscape, a landscape that is willing to be shaped by the effect of the water. His own verse seems to be similarly affected. Notice, for example, how many examples there are of run-on lines, of irregular stops within the lines. Auden speaks at one point of 'these springs/That spurt out everywhere' and that exactly represents one of the effects in the poem of the verse-structure.

New developments, new perspectives, will suddenly be picked up within the lines as if Auden were intent on constantly surprising us. In his poem written 'At the Grave of Henry James' (57) Auden praises the quality of deliberate and disciplined complexity in James. He sees it as a gift to civilisation, commending James for supplying the element of surprise which his own poetry provides. The poem offers also yet another example of Auden's fondness for the long verse-sentence form.

In contrast, look at his poem 'In Memory of W.B. Yeats' (44) where once again he writes in memory of and admiration for a great writer. Part I of this poem is full of abrupt statements, self-contained verses with few examples of run-on lines. The poem also contains some useful examples of the fondness that Auden also had for the epigrammatic phrase, the neat aphorism, an expression of wisdom. He obviously enjoyed writing, for example, that

> The words of a dead man
> Are modified in the guts of the living.

In our section on imagery, mention was made to his constant use of images from war and, in the second stanza of this part of the poem, he seems to relish introducing several separate aspects of such a war: he talks about the revolution within Yeats's own physical system, of the way 'the squares of his mind were empty'—an image which reflects the way in which citizens would desert a city under attack.

Within this poem we are also provided with further evidence of

Auden's versatility in verse. For he provides in Part III a verse-form that closely resembles that employed in the writing of traditional epitaphs. The first stanza, indeed, is a perfect example of the form. In the other stanzas he uses the form a little more loosely but still maintaining the rhyming couplet throughout. In further contrast to something as obviously 'poetic' as the rhyming couplet, Auden provides us with verse that is intentionally prosaic. The outstanding example of this is another poem 'In Memory': his epitaph to 'The Unknown Citizen' is written in a form that is exactly suited to the anonymous person it celebrates. It is bare of any ornamentation other than that of a rhyme which demonstrates the sardonic humour in the poem. Auden regrets the system that could produce such an automaton, but he introduces rhyme as his ironic comment on that system. The rhymes are so often quite obviously contrived. His verse at times threatens, in its apparent lack of control, to become 'bad verse' as in the following lines:

And all the reports on his conduct agree
That, in the modern sense of an old-fashioned word,
                                he was a saint,
For in everything he did he served the Greater Community.

Rhythm and metre have been abandoned in order to 'work' that rhyme between 'agree' and 'Community'. You should be able to find further examples of this kind of contrived rhyming. Auden is obviously enjoying the satiric effects of it. In contrast we have the beautiful lyric effects of such a poem as 'Look, stranger' (27) where Auden has devised a verse-form which re-creates the scene delightfully before our eyes.

Mention has already been made, in the specific commentary on this poem in Part 2 of this book (see p.15), of the superb control of the verse in the second stanza of 'Look, stranger'. There the movement of the shingle is created not only by his use of the onomatopoeic 's' but also in the 'sucking' effect created by his play with that word between lines six and seven.

Auden's technical artistry is further illustrated in the series of sonnets that make up his poem 'The Quest' (52). The fourteen lines in each poem are made up in a variety of ways: sometimes we have a poem of two stanzas of four lines followed by two stanzas of three; then we have others with six, six, and two; then three stanzas of three lines followed by one stanza of five, and so on. There may be a danger that the emphasis on devising such a variety might detract from the impression of sincerity, 'to say things', as Auden once suggested 'not because he believes them but because they sound effective'. Auden is obviously enjoying his craftmanship, but his intention is no less serious for all the enjoyment. This can be said, too, about such an apparently trivial poem as 'Miss Gee' (36). Auden once said that 'If I lived under a dictatorship, I'd write children's stories', and 'Miss Gee' reads very much like a macabre story for children. It opens with a line which suggests his narrative intentions: 'Let me tell you a little story.' His verse-form is simple, but it is used to convey a serious problem of loneliness and frustration, of being what he calls 'a total wreck' in social as well as physical terms. Contrast the effect here, for example, with that in the 'Master and Boatswain' in his 'The Sea and the Mirror' (60). There is no doubt that here his intention is anything but serious, and yet he employs a similar form of verse:

> At Dirty Dick's and Sloppy Joe's
> We drank our liquor straight,
> Some went upstairs with Margery,
> And some, alas, with Kate.

The verse in this poem is designed in form and intention so as to suit the minor characters involved. Where Auden deals with major characters from Shakespeare's play, he, like Shakespeare, varies the verse form. There he employs, to use his words from Alonso 'the solemn music' (*Selected Poems*, p.144). This 'solemn music' is one aspect of the versification in Auden's poetry; the 'chuckle' of which he speaks in 'In Praise of Limestone' is another which often provides a lively contrast.

Part 4

Hints for study

Self-examination

Your examination paper will always make use of the poems themselves, the claims made for the poems by W.H. Auden and the claims
made by others, particularly critics, about that poetry. The first point
for attention, then, in coming to study W.H. Auden must be the
poems. There is always a temptation to look at critical literature to see
what others have had to say about the work. You must resist this. You
must read the poetry and see what you can make of it yourself. Try to
establish what you understand by the contents of the poem; make your
own commentary. Make careful notes on your ideas. Do not merely
persuade yourself that you understand what you have read: test your
ideas and judge them critically. Write your thoughts down in an
ordered and organised way.

At the same time there is no need to try to do this with all the poems
and only then to compare your responses with those of others. You
should take a particular poem and approach it 'cold'. Analyse it for
content. Then attempt your own written commentary on it. Then compare your notions and assessment with those received from the summaries and commentaries in Part 3 of these Notes. You can then assess the
validity or otherwise of your own conclusions in the light of such a
comparison. You may also find that one of the critical works quoted in
Part 5 of these Notes will contain some ideas on the poem you have
attempted. Such 'feedback', as it is called, will help you in several
ways. Obviously it will help you to fill material gaps; it will help to provide explanations which you perhaps did not attempt at all, or which,
having attempted them, you found somewhat lacking. In addition to
details of information and explanation of meaning, such feedback will
offer you ideas about the type of comment that is appropriate for the
particular poem being investigated. You will be able to make an estimate of the nature of comments required at this level.

A third gain from this type of comparative technique is that you will
learn how to say what you have to say, to recognise the kind of language you will need to use at this level of critical comment on a text.
Having had this variety of feedback, you can apply what you have
learned to other poems in the selection and, in this way, construct a
sound approach to Auden's work as a whole.

Selecting the poems for special attention

There is an abundant selection of poems in our text. Which ones do you study? That is a problem that these Notes have attempted to solve. The poems selected for attention in Parts 2 and 3 above, and in this part, are those to which you ought to pay particular attention. They have been selected for what they represent: the thought of W.H. Auden and the salient features of his style. Here is a case where it is possible to be prescriptive. You should read all the poems in *Selected Poems* in order to get the full flavour of Auden's poetry. But there is no need to study all of them in detail. Study those which have been singled out for mention in this book. Study them for content, theme, and the various features of style—Auden's use, say, of rhyme, his varying rhythms, his imagery, his symbolism, and his language.

What does your examiner expect?

The answer to this question may appear obvious. The examiner expects you to be able to show that you know W.H. Auden's poetry. The emphasis here is on the word 'know' and on the word 'poetry'. The word 'know' stresses that element in your examination which is called 'recall'. This is the 'lowest common denominator' in all examinations. You demonstrate knowledge of a factual kind. Thus, you show that you know the *content* of any particular poem, or poems, which you choose to discuss. You also show that you have a *close* knowledge of this content by the appropriate use of brief quotations. Such quotations can be used to substantiate claims that you are making about the poem or poems in question. And remember that they have to be both appropriate *and* brief. Read through Parts 2 and 3 of these Notes, and you will find many such examples interspersed within the text. Note, too, that the use of such quotations *is* expected of you in response to questions on set poetry.

The mention of 'poetry' introduces the other element to be stressed. Many candidates feel that they can impress the examiner by demonstrating what they know about critics' comments on the poem. This is not what the examiner wants. He certainly wants 'informed' comments. He wants to see answers that are obviously the outcome of close reading of the poetry and wide reading of the work of critics. But he wants to see that all you have read you have truly 'made your own'.

Within this part of these Notes you will find some suggested answers. Attend to them not only for their contents but also for their layout. It is not a question of using brief quotations and linking them by brief prose contributions of your own; the examiner wants to see that you can adopt a line of argument and argue it coherently and cohesively, and substantiate it by apt quotation.

Writing your essay

The comments that follow here apply to both course work which acts as a necessary preparation for your examination, and the writing of an examination answer. You should apply yourself rigorously to the writing of essays on books set for study for your examination. It is not sufficient merely to read commentaries or summaries or specimen answers; nor is it sufficient to write copious notes in preparation. The writing of an essay helps to formulate and fix those many ideas and impressions that presented themselves as you studied your subject. Until you do try to give these impressions formal expression you will never make them fully your own. By writing an essay you will be able to give them precision, to select or reject material, and to organise ideas coherently. Writing essays helps you to sort out your ideas, and in so doing, facilitate your learning.

In attempting to answer an examination question a candidate must first assure himself or herself that each part of that question can be handled. Too often, the examiner's experience is that the candidate deals with only part of a question and ignores parts that are equally important. You should take your cue from the question as it is set, and put any preconceived ideas aside. The reading of the question must, in each instance, be careful. While not a piece of great verse this simple jingle does supply very sound advice:

> Be cool, collected, calm and concise,
> Read every question carefully twice.

Planning an answer

No matter how astute your preparation for such an examination may be it is rare that the wording of a question or paper will exactly coincide with any you have previously experienced. It is always a serious error to try to force the new question into a shape that is simply not there, and to try merely to re-present the answers you have provided in the past to 'similar' questions. It is essential in the examination room to spend some five minutes or so outlining your approach to an understanding of the question set.

Specimen questions on the poetry of W.H. Auden

(1) What have you found appealing in Auden's poetry?
(2) From your reading of Auden's poetry what is your understanding of his view of society?

(3) How far are you surprised by the view that Auden 'has no universally accepted masterpieces'?

(4) 'Auden's younger readers today show some tendency to be bored by the social and political concerns of the Thirties, and to question their permanent interest in poetic themes'. Discuss this statement.

(5) How useful is the description of Auden as 'a religious poet'?

(6) Examine the dramatic element in Auden's work.

(7) 'He writes to entertain and instruct as well as to produce the more subtle and profound effects of poetry.' Discuss this statement.

(8) Consider the opinion that it is impossible to take Auden seriously.

(9) Examine Auden's use of nature in his poetry.

(10) 'A religious poet who is also a clown, a virtuoso who is incorrigibly didactic, a satirist who is also a musician and a lyricist.' Discuss this assessment of W.H. Auden.

(11) Auden once said, 'What no critic seems to see in my work are its comic undertones.' Why do you think critics have not recognised them?

(12) 'It is the social aspect of W.H. Auden's verse that will ensure him an enduring and central place among major twentieth-century poets.' Discuss this statement.

(13) 'My poetry doesn't change from place to place, it changes with the years.' What differences have you noticed between an 'early' Auden poem and one written later in his life?

Specimen answers

QUESTION 11: Auden once said, 'What no critic seems to see in my work are its comic undertones.' Why do you think critics have not recognised them?

PLAN: Appropriateness of Auden's phrase 'comic undertones'?
Examples of comic poems/references which are explicit, for example, Miss Gee?
More subtle evidence of comic effect—use of satire—light verse-forms —comic references, for example 'In Praise of Limestone'.
Reasons for critics' 'serious' estimate of Auden—Auden's 'public voice'; his preaching; love and nature in his poetry.

The comedy in Auden's poetry can at times be quite blatant. There is no disguising it, nor is there an obvious wish on Auden's part to do so. His facility with comic verse can be illustrated, for example, by that startling stanza from the 'Master and Boatswain' part of 'The Sea and the Mirror':

> At Dirty Dick and Sloppy Joe's
>   We drank our liquor straight,
> Some went upstairs with Margery,
>   And some, alas, with Kate.

The silly sentiments combine with the jingle of the verse to create a comic effect. The verse is not unlike that which he devised to tell the story of Miss Gee, a sad spinster who never knew love, but lived instead a lonely life relieved only by the fantasies she enjoyed in her dreams. Her sad and lonely life is ended abruptly by cancer. The ending of the poem is both macabre and ironic—macabre in its detail of how the surgeon 'cut Miss Gee in half' and ironic in that only when she is dead do the secrets of her body become known to men.

One critic has called Auden 'a clown' and this is a role he frequently likes to assume in his poetry. In one poem, 'Forty Years On' he becomes Autolycus, a comic character out of Shakespeare's play, *A Winter's Tale*. Autolycus is one who, as he says himself, is 'a snapper up of unconsidered trifles'. He is a kind of confidence-trickster who makes his living by his wits. One line from the poem may well be seen as applying to Auden's own poetic output:

> all I had
> was the courtier's agility to adapt
> my rogueries to the times.

Sometimes Auden perhaps feels the need to present his humour in just this kind of unsubtle way. In such cases, he can hardly speak of 'comic undertones' without being open to the charge of understating his case! It may well be that, given such obvious humour, he could expect his readers and critics to look for a vein of humour in what may often appear a deeply serious poem.

One such poem might be 'The Unknown Citizen'. Obviously the state of affairs which is suggested by the poem's subject is a deplorable one. We know that one major theme in Auden's poetry is that of the need for individual identity. He constantly demands the right for each individual to be himself and not merely be a part of a mechanical system. That being the case, this poem can be seen as an oblique attack on such a system. Yet, in addition to this, it is obvious, too, that the poet has enjoyed writing the poem. He obviously admires his own ingenuity. And, in devising the epigraph in which he dedicates the poem to 'JS/07/M/378', he provides that extra sardonic touch.

The poem 'Refugee Blues' deals with an equally bitter topic, the persecution of the Jews. The subject, however, as the title itself suggests, is given a musical framework. There is a suggestion of a refrain in the last line of each stanza which reinforces this light, musical effect. We might say that such a form for such a subject was in bad taste. Be that as it may, even this poem does serve to illustrate the presence of 'comic undertones'.

In one of his best-known poems 'In Praise of Limestone' we can sense the comic effect searching to be recognised. The poem is, again, an appeal for individualism. Through the analogy of a landscape composed of a stone that allows itself to change and be changed, as it were, Auden appeals for that sense of the individual that will add variety to life. His intention is serious, but there is still room for the sense of the ridiculous. We have, for instance, that delightful depiction of a god having 'temper tantrums', which can only be assuaged or softened by 'a good lay'. Auden's audacity is everywhere in evidence, and its effect is often comic. Nevertheless, it is not too difficult to appreciate, to quote partially from this same poem, 'how evasive is [his] humour' for those critics of whom he complains.

Much of Auden's poetry is demonstrably serious, and serious to the exclusion of any suggestion of humour. He speaks in an essay on poetry of 'two kinds of art' one of which is 'escape art' and the other is 'parable art, that art which shall teach man to unlearn hatred and learn love'. In this last phrase, Auden indicates that there is a strong didactic line in his poetry. Such poems as 'Spain' or 'In Time of War' illustrate well this other Auden in whom the clown is silent. The latter poem, particularly, is full of large, impressive gestures such as 'Only happiness is shared/And anger, and the idea of love' or 'The life of man is never quite completed,' or 'We have no destiny assigned us'. And, further than this, there are those serious love poems of his like 'Lay your sleeping head, my love' which has been called the greatest love poem in this century. There are no 'comic undertones' there, any more than there are 'comic undertones' in the idyllic description of nature captured in 'Look, stranger, at this island now'.

It may be that such private intensity here and such a public voice elsewhere have both conspired to drown the effect of the 'comic undertones' which he wanted to be recognised.

QUESTION 12: 'It is the social aspect of W.H. Auden's verse that will ensure him an enduring and central place among major twentieth-century poets.' Discuss this statement.

The immediate focus for such a statement is, no doubt, Auden's writing during the 1930s. The poems of this period deal with the various political threats to society as he knew it. One of the most significant events of the 1930s, in political terms, was the civil war in Spain. This was a war which appealed to the emotions and sympathies of many writers and artists who joined the fight against the fascist side. Auden, in fact, was employed mainly as a writer of propaganda, and he was largely dissatisfied with that role. He spoke of 'the flat ephemera' pamphlet'—the symbol of propaganda—in his poem 'Spain'. This poem, written in 1937, has, as its title demonstrates, the war in Spain as its subject. 'Madrid is the heart', he writes, thereby suggesting the notion of its being the centre both of operations and of emotions. But emotions, he tells us, are only expressed now in 'the ambulance and the sandbag'. All is evidence of what he refers to as 'the struggle'. It is a struggle which hopes for fruition, for the establishment of a true democracy where we may see, for example,

> The eager election of chairmen
> By the sudden forest of hands.

But it is a time like that of which he speaks in his 'In Time of War', when 'we lie in the present's unopened sorrow'. The social evil that is war is spoken of, again, in his poem 'Refugee Blues' which tells of one of the tragedies of war, namely, the creation of a loss of identity, the creation of a state where 'If you've got no passport you're officially dead'. This poem is full of such dramatic statements which are histrionic in their effect. It is one of the features of Auden's social verse that may well ensure him future esteem when he is ranked among poets of this century. However, Auden himself was in the end not sure of the value of such poems as 'Spain'. Indeed, he described it bluntly as 'trash'. One major criticism of the poem is that it is so bluntly propagandist that it loses its force as a poem. In that case it could be seen to be as 'flat' and 'ephemeral' as is the pamphleteering of which Auden spoke. There is, indeed, a considerable amount of rhetoric in the poem, of carefully balances phrases, of telling repetition as in the constant reiteration of 'But today the struggle,' or of contrived images like that which describes Spain as 'that arid square . . . soldered so crudely to inventive Europe'.

This poem, and those others which speak of political ills and oppression, voice conviction—in what is often powerful verse. His attack, for example, on the complacency which could lead to such a disaster is scathing and compelling:

> For the fears which made us respond
> To the medicine ad. and the brochure of winter cruises
> Have become invading battalions.

The final line shatters the reader's complacency. The banalities of the 'medicine ad.' and 'the brochure' create an awareness of the trivial concerns the preoccupy us whilst more significant events are ignored.

Auden's social concerns, however, are not always expressed in such large contexts as war. The mention of the banalities in the lines quoted above prompt us to remember other poems which concentrate on social themes. One thing that particularly perturbs him is the threat of loneliness in society for the individual. He talks of man as 'Being alone' and of being 'the frightened soul'. He is concerned that, given the large framework of society, such loneliness will become more and more a modern disease. One poem which expresses his concern most poignantly is 'Miss Gee'. This tells of a lonely spinster who never knew love and whose only contribution to life was as a corpse in the dissecting room. The verse-form that is adopted may not be his most ambitious or technically inventive but, in its simplicity and lack of colour, it exactly reflects the character of whom he speaks.

The social disease of loneliness in 'Miss Gee' is but one example of the social aspects of Auden's verse. The notion of disease is a frequent one in his verse and in an earlier poem he speaks of sanatoria where diseases of all kinds can be catered for. These, he suggests, are under threat in a society which is perceived as becoming less and less sympathetic to imperfections in its citizens. His immediate reference may have been to the movements he recognised in contemporary Germany, which led eventually to the persecution of the Jews with which 'Refugee Blues' deals.

This kind of atmosphere demands 'conformity' and this, too, provides the subject for another theme in Auden's social verse. He rejects the notion of conformity and applauds individualism and its manifestations. His telling satire on conformity, 'The Unknown Citizen', is certainly a piece of verse which will ensure him 'an enduring place'. It is a masterful combination of the grossly banal in terminology—'Yet he wasn't a scab or odd in his views'—and the technical wizardry that shows us the poet enjoying his craft.

Auden's social verse is, however, not always so blunt. The poem which he described as his favourite is 'In Praise of Limestone', a brilliant allegory; in it Auden speaks of his admiration for a landscape that is not predictable, that can boast several different, and even eccentric, forms. It is a living symbol of resistance to conformity in society, a conformity that would submerge the individual. Ironically, he takes to task the poet who insists on being pragmatic, on calling 'the sun the sun' and who finds the limestone landscape disturbing as evidence of something more truly poetic.

QUESTION 13: 'My poetry doesn't change from place to place, it changes with the years.' What differences have you noticed between an 'early' Auden poem and one written later in his life?

The two poems which lend themselves most easily for contrast in this context of time are 'Look, stranger, at this island now' which was written in 1935, and 'River Profile', written in 1966. They recommend themselves for such a study in contrasts, ironically enough, because of their common subject. They both describe what could be called a 'waterscape' as distinct from the landscapes for which Auden is so well known.

The first poem is lyrical in many of its effects. The invitation is to look at a pleasing scene where 'The leaping light for your delight discovers' a view which the poet finds quite beautiful. We see, in the opening stanza of the poem, Auden's play with the liquid 'l' sound, an effect which persists into the second stanza. We notice, too, the introduction of other poetic tricks which help create a sense of movement. The use of 'swaying' in the line 'The swaying sound of the sea' evokes this effect of movement, and it is reinforced in the second stanza by his use of a run-on line where the word-shapes themselves enact the movement in the scene:

> And the shingle scrambles after the suck –
> ing surf

The word 'sucking' is split and part of it is moved into the next line to suggest exactly that movement. His use of the word 'scrambles' creates an amusing effect which helps suggest still further that the poet is enjoying the experience.

One further poetic device that the poet employs with obvious relish is that of onomatopoeia. This is a technique which helps to create an effect of sound by the use of consonants. Here the suck of the sea, its soft swishing sound, is represented in Auden's employment of repetitive 's' sounds which cumulatively create the sibilance of the sea. It is a hushed, untroubled and untroubling sound. This helps to provide the idyllic environment Auden wishes to hold up for our admiration. These sounds, he hopes, 'May wander like a river' through our sensory experience. The river evoked by that image is far removed from that in his later 'River Profile'. The quiet hush of his first river is immediately destroyed in the opening stanza of this second. It finds its origin in quite another environment, and, according to Auden is the product of 'thundering head-on collisions of cloud and rock'.

The poem is written as a satire on the usual romantic view of the course of a river. The landscapes through which it travels are far from idyllic and are mostly industrial areas where the various effluents visibly affect the river: 'it changes colour'. There are still times when 'its progress' is 'regal' and we have a brief glimpse of them in the poem. But the trees only provide a suggestion of an idyll quickly destroyed by the onset of chimneys! In such an environment 'it puts off majesty'.

The contrast in scene is not the only difference between 'River Profile' and the earlier poem. The language that helps to create the scene has changed dramatically. The movement in the first poem created by words suggestive of delight now takes a harsher form where the river 'plunges ram-stam'. The word 'plunges' may suggest more haste, or even a sense of recklessness and lack of control. The word 'ram-stam' is designed to suit the industrial environment. It can be seen as a pollution of the language itself. But the haste and plunging effect are not designed by the poet to create any sense of awe such as we were expected to experience in the first poem. Instead, the poem is full of pessimism. It is accelerating through life, lowering itself, losing all sense of grace, until eventually, as Auden puts it, the river 'wearies to its final act of surrender'.

His first poem ends on a much more optimistic note. Life will be untroubled. The vessels out at sea will 'all the summer through the water saunter'. The river in poetry is often a symbol for the course of life, and the river in the first poem stands for a rhythm of life which allows people to develop, to shape their own individual lives.

Auden's earlier poetry made constant appeals for this kind of liberty. His later poetry seems to be more cynical. In his 'In Memory of W.B. Yeats' he said 'Poetry makes nothing happen'. That was written in 1939. Perhaps the evidence of the Second World War demonstrated the impotence of the poet in the modern world. The epigraph for the poem 'River Profile' says that 'Our body is a moulded river' and may well suggest that the conformity Auden had always abhorred had now become too much of a reality for him. It is the tone of the two poems that perhaps provides the greatest contrast between the early and the later Auden.

Suggestions for further reading

The text

AUDEN, W.H.: *Selected Poems*, edited by Edward Mendelson, Faber and Faber, London and Boston, 1979.

The arrangement of poems in this edition is chronological, and critical approaches to Auden are also often chronological. Thus critics speak of Auden's 'early' period, of his 'poetry of the Thirties', of his 'middle period', and of his 'late' poetry. This chronological emphasis can lead to a treatment of the poems which classifies them as less good, say, because they belong to an 'early' or 'late' period, whilst if they belong to the Thirties they are more to be admired. It is wiser to avoid this impressionistic approach and to judge each poem on its own merit.

Other works by W.H. Auden

To gain a fuller appreciation of Auden's attitude towards poetry it is worth reading his collection of essays, *The Dyer's Hand and other Essays*, published by Faber and Faber, London, 1963.

The poems in *Selected Poems* are drawn from various single volumes of Auden's poetry, and Edward Mendelson, who has edited this selection of Auden's verse, supplies a useful list of sources on page 305 in the set text.

Biography

HOGGART, RICHARD: *W.H. Auden*, Longman, London, 1957. A brief biographical and critical study. A useful introduction. ′

OSBORNE, CHARLES: *W.H. Auden, The Life of a Poet*, Eyre Methuen, London, 1980. A delightful study of Auden's life and friends.

Criticism

BLAIR, J.G.: *The Poetic Art of W.H. Auden*, Princeton University Press, Princeton, New Jersey, 1965.

BUELL, F.: *W.H. Auden as a Social Poet*, Cornell University Press, Ithaca, New York, 1974. A study of many aspects of Auden's social concerns in his early and later poetry.

FORD, BORIS (ED.): *The Modern Age*, Pelican Guide to English Literature, Penguin Books, Harmondsworth, pp.377–94. A general essay on the poetry of Auden which offers some provocative views of the poet.

FULLER, JOHN: *A Reader's Guide to W.H. Auden*, Thames and Hudson, London, 1970. An invaluable guide to individual poems.

HOGGART, RICHARD: *Auden, An Introductory Essay*, Chatto and Windus, London 1965. A more recent critical study of the poet which brings the commentaries up to date with later poems.

SPEARS, MONROE K.: *The Poetry of W.H. Auden*, Oxford University Press, New York, 1963. One of the classic studies of the poet's work, well worth reading.

SPEARS, MONROE K. (ED.): *Auden, A Collection of Critical Essays* (Twentieth Century Views), Prentice-Hall (Spectrum Books), New Jersey, 1964.

The author of these notes

DOMINIC HYLAND was educated at the Universities of Cambridge, Manchester and Lancaster. He has taught English in schools, Colleges and Polytechnics, as well as with the Universities of Liverpool, Lancaster and the Open University. He has examined English Literature at Ordinary and Advanced Levels for the G.C.E., and is currently Chief Examiner in English Literature with one of the largest Examining Boards in the country. He has written five York Notes as well as a variety of other Study Aids in Literature and English Language.